JUST CLEAN ENOUGH

Make Peace with Sort-of-Spotless and **Find More Time for You**

365 EASY TIDYING TIPS

I. B. Caruso and **Jenny Schroedel**

adamsmedia

Avon, Massachusetts

Published by Adams Media,
a division of F+W Media, Inc.
57 Littlefield Street,
Avon, MA 02322. U.S.A.
www.adamsmedia.com

Contains material adapted and
abridged from *The Everything® Home
Storage Solutions Book* by Iyna Bort
Caruso, copyright © 2007 by F+W
Media, Inc., ISBN 10: 1-59337-662-
6, ISBN 13: 978-1-59337-662-8; *The
Everything® Organize Your Home
Book, 2nd Edition* by Jenny Schroedel,
copyright © 2008, 2002 by F+W
Media, Inc., ISBN 10: 1-59869-393-X,
ISBN 13: 978-1-59869-393-5.

ISBN 10: 1-4405-0656-6
ISBN 13: 978-1-4405-0656-7
eISBN 10: 1-4405-1065-2
eISBN 13: 978-1-4405-1065-6

Printed in the United States of
America.

10 9 8 7 6 5 4 3 2 1

**Library of Congress Cataloging-in-
Publication Data**
Caruso, I. B.
Just clean enough / I. B. Caruso and
Jenny Schroedel.
p. cm.
Includes index.
ISBN-13: 978-1-4405-0656-7
ISBN-10: 1-4405-0656-6
ISBN-13: 978-1-4405-1065-6 (ebk)
ISBN-10: 1-4405-1065-2 (ebk)
1. House cleaning. 2. Orderliness.
3. Housekeeping. I. Schroedel, Jenny.
II. Title.
TX324.C377 2010
648'.5—dc22
2010038808

*This book is available at quantity
discounts for bulk purchases.
For information, please call
1-800-289-0963.*

CONTENTS

Introduction

KICK PERFECTION TO THE CURB

Your home is a mess, but you're probably not a candidate for *Hoarders*, so no worries! Forget perfection or shame or guilt. The title of this book isn't *Everything Must Be Perfect* or *You're a Horrible, Lazy Human Being*. You have a life, and while it runs more smoothly when you know where things are, you don't have extra time or the inclination to spend the time you do have cleaning and organizing. And the good news is *you don't have to*. Inside are hundreds of quick, easy—emphasis on *easy*—ways to keep your home feeling fresh without wasting too much valuable time or energy.

After all, this is home organization, not boot camp! The desk in your home office doesn't have to be clean enough to eat off of. Your kids' rooms don't have to be spotless, and frankly, no matter what you do, they never will be. Since you're not competing for a Most Perfect Home award, it makes sense to focus less on organizing and sanitizing and more on keeping your sanity. You'll be glad you did.

Toss It, Already!

Clutter is Public Enemy #1 in the quest for creating a sane sanctuary, so you'll have to get into the habit of taking inventory of your stuff. You know the drill: Toss, Keep, and Donate. Of course, you're trying to clear off your kitchen table, not fill a dump truck with the contents of your living room, but deciding what you actually need vs. what you can let go of may still feel like a daunting task. Fortunately, it's simpler than you may think. Use the following guidelines to clear out whatever's lurking and you'll feel lighter in an instant.

1. If you can't remember the last time you used, wore, or played with something, get rid of it. That "someday I might need this" philosophy is a throwback to your grandma's era, so let it go.
2. When debating about something that holds sentimental value, separate the object from the memory. If the memory is strong, do you really need the object?
3. If it's broken, toss it.
4. If you uncover duplicates, donate the extra.

Don't revert to your packrat ways once you've started sorting. A painless investment of ten or fifteen minutes of daily touchups is all it takes to keep you from burning cookies while you search for an oven mitt amidst kitchen rubble, or preventing your preschooler from being late to school as you try to track down a lone shoe in a swamped closet.

Forget the White Glove Test . . .

. . . but consider the cleaning part of this equation. Because being organized is important, but it's not everything. Like it or not, to get that "There's no place like home" feeling, some cleaning is involved. Again, we're not pushing perfection. Dirt is a part of life, and you don't have to spend every night scrubbing floors and corralling dust. But you are going to have to wash your dishes, keep up with laundry, and get rid of the ring around your toilet. Otherwise, you risk staring at a dirty floor in a panic ten minutes before your in-laws show up—and no one wants that! Don't fret: the tips inside will have you sitting pretty while the dust settles.

This Book's Breakdown

You're a smart person and chances are you already know what you need to do to get your home in order. We'll show you how to take all that info and work it into your lifestyle. You know the expression "Take it one day at a time"? Here the expression is more like, "Take it five minutes at a time." This will be your motto as you work your way through this book. Each task has a completion time; that way, you can decide what to do depending on how much time you have available. Say you have twenty minutes to get some organizing done. Flip through the book and find a twenty-minute task. There's also a chapter for every room in your home, and each chapter is broken down into the days of the week, with a different task and tip for each day. If you want to start your cleanup in your bathroom, jump to Chapter 1 and follow the week-by-week plan for that room.

Go Forth and Conquer

No matter how you use this book, remember you won't get the results you want by trying to be perfect. Instead, clean the way you want, *when you want*, and make your house the home it was meant to be—one that's comfortable and makes you feel good about how you live . . . even if it means you sometimes coexist with the dust bunnies under the couch.

WHO'S AFRAID OF THE BIG, BAD BATHROOM?

The bathroom: everyone's least favorite room to clean. Honestly, they're not that bad. Bathrooms are among the smaller rooms in the house, and they generally don't attract much clutter that doesn't belong there. But with all the toiletries, linens, and cleaning products that can accumulate, it's a space that can easily get out of control—and fast! It's also the place where you begin and end your day, so it deserves a little of your time and attention. Who wants to wake up to messes, mold, and mildew, right?

Monday: Time to Purge

🕐 **20 minutes**

If you're like most people, you have toiletries in your bathroom you don't use, don't remember buying, and possibly can't even identify. The time to purge has come. Start by laying an old towel on the floor; this will be your staging area. Next, go through every product in your bathroom, from soap and shampoo to medication and makeup. Separate items into three piles on the towel: Toss, Keep, and Donate. If you find an item that you use regularly, keep it. If something is perfectly good but just didn't work out for you (a body wash that you're allergic to, for example), consider giving it to a friend or family member who will use it. If something is old and crusty, or only a drop remains in the bottle, toss it! You'll get over the loss in due time.

Tuesday: Put It Back

🕐 **20 minutes**

Before you start putting items back in their old places, stop and consider the best way to reorganize. Keep the items you use regularly as well as some first-aid products you might need to get to quickly in your medicine cabinet so they'll be on hand. If you have kids, make sure all medications are in childproof containers and stored on high shelves for extra safety. Take boxed items out of their original packages, where appropriate, to free up space. As for the items you pulled out of your other cabinets and drawers, do they all need to return there? With the exception of a few rolls, bulky items like toilet paper might be better stored elsewhere, such as in a linen closet in the hallway.

Wednesday: Attention, Ladies!

🕐 15 minutes

Makeup and hair products are usually the biggest culprits when it comes to bathroom mayhem. If your makeup, moisturizers, combs, hair products, blow dryer, and other assorted tools are in a heap on your vanity, then you have some work to do. First, attack your makeup. Do you really need all this stuff? If there are old, dried-out, used-up lipsticks, bottles of nail polish, or anything else in the pile, throw them away. The keepers should be placed neatly in a drawer or makeup bag that is stashed out of sight. Next, go through all your hair products. Which of them do you use on a daily basis, and what products have you tried once or twice but haven't touched since? Toss the latter and find a good place for the former, such as a clear shelf or empty cabinet.

Almost Perfect

Believe it or not, makeup—yes, even the expensive kind—has a shelf life. According to the FDA, "Cosmetic products are generally formulated and tested for a shelf life of 1 to 3 years." You don't need to bust out your label maker, but if you come across a rarely used eyeliner that's getting a little crusty around the edges, don't hesitate to trash it.

Thursday: Keep First-Aid Items Handy

🕐 15 minutes

Before you get all carried away throwing out old and unwanted toiletries and putting things away in an orderly fashion, remember that there are some items you absolutely need to keep at the ready. We're talking about first-aid items: adhesive bandages, antibacterial ointments, pain relievers, rubbing alcohol and/or hydrogen peroxide, cotton balls, and so on. Make sure these items are well stocked, not old or expired, and in a location where you can grab them quickly. This might be in a basket on a shelf or in the medicine cabinet. Finally, when you run out of something, don't wait to replace it; you never know when a need will arise.

Friday: Give Your Tub a Bath

🕐 5 minutes

About to hop in the shower and give yourself a scrub? Why not do the same for your tub? Cleaning the tub while you're in it anyway is a great way to lessen the pain of bathroom maintenance. Just be sure you're using an all-natural, odorless cleaner; you don't want to pass out from toxic fumes and hit your head on the faucet. Then someone else will have a mess to clean up! Or, if you're taking a bath instead of a shower, just dump about a quarter of a box of baking soda into your bathwater; this will soothe your sore muscles and clean the tub at the same time.

Almost Perfect

A squeegee is a great way to prevent bathroom moisture from turning into hard-to-remove mold and mildew. Just keep one in a cabinet or drawer near the tub, and squeegee the tile walls and/or glass doors after every shower. The squeegee will wipe the water off the walls and send it down the drain where it belongs.

Saturday: Find Shower Items a Good Home

🕐 10 minutes

Now that your tub is clean and you've recycled all those nearly empty shampoo bottles and thrown away those slivers of old soap, start fresh with a new organizational system. Corner shelves in the tub area help you to recoup lost space and maintain a clean look. No-tool stacking systems and over-the-showerhead shelving units are other ways to streamline the parade of plastic bottles that give even the neatest of bathrooms a sloppy look. Besides, bottles that sit on a damp tub ledge encourage the growth of mold by trapping water underneath the containers. House them on higher, drier ground and you'll head off the problem before it even begins.

Sunday: Create More Storage Space

🕐 30 minutes

Now that you've cleaned the bathroom and rid yourself of all those old, unused products, you have a better idea of what your true bathroom needs are. If you still find you need more storage space, take a few measurements and then head out to your local home goods store. Over-the-toilet shelving is a great way to bring more storage to a small bathroom. Apothecary jars offer an attractive way to store items that don't have a logical home, such as cotton balls and hair accessories. Install a peg or two on the wall by the sink for hairdryers and curling irons. They take up way too much space in a drawer. Wall-mounted hairdryers, often seen in hotel rooms, are another alternative.

Bathroom Week 2

Monday: Get Mold Under Control

🕐 20 minutes

Got mold? Don't take it personally. Because the space is often small and not well ventilated, mold is a problem in many bathrooms. If there is mold growing on your shower walls or ceiling, it's time to take action. Lucky for you, there's a quick fix. There are many spray-and-leave cleaners you can buy for your shower, or you can prepare a solution of ¼ cup bleach and one quart water at home. Spray the moldy area with the solution and leave it for ten minutes, then wipe down the surface with a damp sponge. Voila! You can reduce mold in the future by keeping a window open—especially when showering—or by installing a ventilation fan, which will clear out moist air and prevent mold and mildew.

Tuesday: Tackle the Kids' Bathroom

🕐 30 minutes

For a children's bathroom, begin the same way you did for other bathrooms in your house. Purge old products and clean out cabinets and shelves. Once you have things reduced to the necessities, employ some organizational items to keep things neat. An over-the-door shoe holder with plastic pockets is ideal for holding washcloths, powders, and bathing products. Put up a few attractive hooks on the back of the bathroom door for bathrobes, pajamas, and wet towels. Hooks make it easier for kids to hang things up, which gives them less of an excuse to toss items on the floor. Dedicate a place for bath toys. Baskets work really well. Otherwise, toys wind up underfoot and are liable to become safety hazards. Speaking of hazards, childproof any cabinets you don't want your kids to access and use only unbreakable containers—never glass—in the bathroom.

Wednesday: Prepare for Guests

🕐 15 minutes

If you're expecting out-of-town visitors anytime soon, you'll want to get your guest bathroom in shape for the occasion. If you don't have a guest bathroom, that's all the more reason to prepare your regular bathroom for their arrival. Make sure you have clean towels and washcloths available, and place a full bottle of hand soap on the sink. If you want to add an extra touch, fill a decorative basket with travel-size toiletries: toothpaste, soap, shampoo, conditioner, and lotion. This will give your guests the comfort of staying in a hotel while still feeling at home. And this should go without saying, but make sure the bathroom is clean before your friends or family members arrive. Mold and grime are not for your guests' eyes!

Thursday: Consider the Shower Curtain

🕐 15 minutes

Take a look at your shower curtain. Does anything strike you? If you have a nasty mold situation, torn shower curtain ring holes, or a shower curtain you just dislike, now's the time to start fresh. If your shower curtain is in decent shape, take it down and give it a quick wash. If you don't care for it or if it's discolored, have fun shopping for a more decorative curtain to hang outside your tub. If your shower curtain liner is moldy, throw that sucker away and replace it with a sturdy, mildew-resistant shower curtain liner. These liners really work and can cut your cleaning time way down. Going forward, pick up a bottle of shower cleaner—or just use watered-down bleach—and spray on the inside of the curtain after each use to keep mold at bay.

Friday: Try a New Approach

🕐 5 minutes

If you find that your bathroom is overflowing with cleaning products that you don't use, why not try something different?

When you're shopping for new bathroom cleaning products, consider purchasing an all-purpose cleaner that you can use on multiple surfaces to avoid creating clutter. You might also try a toilet bowl cleaner that resides in your toilet tank and does the work for you every time you flush. Only purchase items you know you will use, and look for the all-natural, nontoxic variety if possible.

Saturday: Consolidate Cleaning Products

🕐 15 minutes

With issues like soap scum to toilet stains and everything in between, your bathroom can be a funky place. And, whether or not you use them, chances are you already have some cleaning products and tools in your bathroom. Take a few minutes to assess the situation in the cabinet under the bathroom sink. Is it clogged with cleaners you don't use, empty bottles from ones you've used up, or filthy rags and scraggly old toothbrushes? If so, it's time to get back to basics. Toss all empty, ancient, or otherwise useless cleaning products. Gather up any dirty towels or rags to be laundered. Wipe down the inside of the cabinet and load your keeper items back in.

Almost Perfect

Keep your cleaning supplies in caddies and keep a caddy in each room that you clean. For example, keep all of your bathroom supplies in a caddy under the sink so you're not wasting time looking for supplies when you could be cleaning.

Sunday: See the Light

🕐 **30 minutes**

Nothing makes a bathroom look clean and new like good lighting. If you have fluorescent fixtures, consider using bulbs that have a warmer glow. To create a look that you love, think about the time of day when the light most appeals to you. Some people love the bright morning sun, while others enjoy the mellow afternoon light. You can even out the lighting around a mirror by placing a sconce on either side of it. If you're feeling especially inspired, you can increase the coziness of your tub or shower by installing a recessed fixture that is designed to withstand moisture. If your bathroom is often chilly, you might want to place a heat lamp over the shower or tub.

Bathroom Week 3

Monday: Dust in the Bathroom? Believe It!

🕐 **5 minutes**

Take a closer look at the top of the toilet tank, the vanity, and the mirror. These are all surfaces that can attract dust, and no one wants a fuzzy toilet. Fortunately, there are numerous products on the market that make dusting a snap, from Swiffer brand dusters to Endust air dusters and cleaning wipes. You can even just grab some toilet paper and give these surfaces a wipe-down. If you take a few minutes once a week, you'll find that the dust doesn't have time to accumulate. This simple step can give your bathroom a brighter, cleaner look in almost no time flat.

Tuesday: Show Your Linens Some Love

$\bigodot$ 20 minutes

Today take a few minutes to survey one of the key components of your bathroom: the linens. First, check out your towels and washcloths. Are they worn, stained, or not very absorbent? If so, consider investing in some new, high-quality replacements. If your bathmat is looking a little rough—filthy, frayed, or otherwise past its prime—pick up a new one of those as well. Make sure all of the new linens you buy are machine washable and of a high enough quality that the colors won't bleed or fade after only a few washings.

Almost Perfect

Clean, neat towels are a super important addition to a clean bathroom, but who can remember when they were last washed or whose towels are who's—especially in a home with kids. To save time and keep your towels fresh either use all white towels and bleach them each week, or assign each family member a towel color.

Wednesday: Treat Yourself to a Trashcan

$\bigodot$ 20 minutes

Most people think that a bathroom trashcan should be tiny. Why? Who knows. But for some families, a pint-sized trashcan simply isn't sufficient. If you find that you're emptying your bathroom trash every few days, save yourself some time and get yourself a new, larger trashcan. Consider getting one with a lid so you don't have to stare at your used tissues and cotton swabs every time you're in the bathroom. Also, if you don't already do so, keep a plastic bag in your trashcan. Not only will this keep the can clean, but it will also allow you to seal off the germs when you empty the trash. Finally, keep a spray disinfectant on hand and spray the can each time you change the bag.

Thursday: Bring in the Beauty

🕐 10 minutes

A great way to liven up your bathroom is to add some decorations. You don't have to spend a lot of money—in fact, some items can be swiped from other areas of your home. For instance, hang a framed photo or painting to bring some color to the walls; just make sure the glass in the frame is tight against the piece so it doesn't warp. Also consider adding a potted plant or two to your bathroom. While the warm, moist atmosphere can make mold a challenge, this climate can also be an opportunity to try out some tropical plants—orchids, for example—that would not necessarily thrive in other parts of the house. However, when adding decorations, use an editing eye. You don't want to clutter up the open spaces in your bathroom with knickknacks or anything that's going to make cleaning more difficult.

Friday: Give Reading Materials a Good Home

🕐 15 minutes

While it's not something we like to admit, many of us get some of our best reading done in the bathroom. Romance novels, tabloid magazines, those little toilet-shaped trivia books . . . who can resist some good bathroom reading material? If those magazines and trivia books are cluttering up your vanity, or worse, scattered on your floor, it's time to get organized. Invest in a wire magazine rack that can be mounted on the wall or a slim one that can sit on the floor without taking up too much space. Also, keep the amount of reading material you store in the bathroom to a minimum. Do you really need last February's issue of *Men's Health* or *Good Housekeeping* sitting around? Clear out older magazines and replace them with the most up-to-date issues, and aim to keep only one or two books in circulation at a time.

Saturday: De-Gunk That Drain

🕐 15 minutes

Got a slow drain? Don't just deal with it—do something! If the water in your tub or sink sticks around too long before draining, you probably have a clog. Luckily, you don't have to hire a plumber to handle this, and you probably don't even need to drop fifteen bucks on a bottle of Drano. Instead, unbend a wire hanger, stick the end down the drain, and gently poke around. You'll probably pull up some lovely looking clumps of wet hair, soap, lint, and a few other surprises. Run the water and see if it goes down more easily. If it's still slow, grab a plunger and give it a few good pumps. That should bring up any remaining obstructions. And in the future, attack that clog before all your showers start turning into baths!

🕐 5 minutes

Since this is a weekend day, we're giving you an extra tip. After you snake your drain, it's important to stop any additional gunk in its tracks. To keep your drains from getting clogged in the first place, buy a drain guard—a wire mesh cup that fits over your shower or sink drain and acts as a filter, preventing stuff like hair and chunks of soap from clogging up your pipes. Just empty it after you shower or use the sink, and you'll be good to go.

Sunday: Rock Out in the Restroom

🕐 **20 minutes**

Let's be honest; you likely spend a lot of time in the bathroom—maybe more than you'd like to admit. You might as well make the time you spend in there as enjoyable as possible by piping in some music. After all, who doesn't like to relax in the tub or rock out while getting ready for a night out? To do this you need a system that's moisture resistant, easy to take care of, and relatively small in size. If a radio is all you need, you might consider purchasing a shower clock radio unit. Not only are these waterproof, but they also have a clock so you'll never take too long in the shower and make yourself late for work. If you would prefer to have a CD or MP3 player in the bathroom, try to find one that can handle the moisture in the room, and make sure it has a cord that can reach the nearest power outlet. Consider a battery-powered device if you're short on outlets or if you simply want a more streamlined, self-contained unit.

Bathroom Week 4

Monday: Hamper Time

🕐 **20 minutes**

If you find that your bathroom is often strewn with pajama bottoms, crumpled pairs of underwear, or any other linens and items of clothing, you're a prime candidate for a hamper. After all, it's just as easy to throw something in a hamper as it is to throw it on the floor. If you think your family could benefit from having a hamper in the bathroom, go to your local home goods store and peruse the offerings. You may select a standard-size hamper with a lid that sits on the floor, or you might go with one that hangs on the back of the door to keep floor space clear. If you have the space, buy two different hampers: one for whites and one for darks. But whatever style you choose, be sure it's big enough to meet your needs. The last thing you need in your newly organized bathroom is an overflowing hamper!

Tuesday: Add Your Favorite Scent

🕐 10 minutes

Bathrooms can get a little dank and smelly from time to time. Luckily, it doesn't take much to keep this room nice and fresh. Try out some scented candles, incense, a plug-in air freshener, or some really fragrant fresh-cut flowers. Choose your favorite scent and then indulge in a few items that you'll enjoy in your bathroom on a daily basis. Perhaps you like the sweet scent of vanilla or the clean fragrance of freshly washed linens. There's a candle in every scent you can imagine out there! You might even add a pump-style bottle of a nicely scented lotion to your vanity or sink for use after you wash your hands. Soap can dry out your skin, so a little moisturizer will be a great touch.

Wednesday: Storing Toilet Paper

🕐 5 minutes

It goes without saying that toilet paper is a necessity in the bathroom, but those rolls can take up a lot of valuable space.

Instead of storing big, bulky packages of toilet paper in the bathroom, try keeping just three or four rolls at a time there, and find a place to store them where they're easily accessible. This doesn't mean you should create a pyramid out of them on top of the toilet tank. If there's a nearby cabinet with some space available, keep them there, or consider purchasing a toilet paper roll holder just for this purpose. These are usually tall plastic tubes with lids that can store up to six rolls of toilet paper at a time. They can slide into the slim space between the toilet and the sink, and the plastic container and lid will keep germs off your clean rolls.

Almost Perfect

We all know what toilet paper is for, but it can also come in handy when you need to do a quick bathroom cleanup job. If you notice that hair and dust are accumulating in the corners of the room, simply grab a wad of toilet paper, dampen it under the faucet, and wipe up the offending clumps. You can use the same method to dust off the toilet tank or wipe up splashes from your shower.

Thursday: Think Outside the Box

🕒 **5 minutes**

Even the most attentive among us can miss some hot spots for germs and grime. A few spots that most people neglect are:

- doorknobs (both inside and outside the bathroom door)
- faucet handles
- the toilet handle

We often touch these places with dirty hands, so pick up a package of disposable disinfectant cleaning cloths and store them in a cabinet or under the sink. Then, every once in a while, give those germ-attracting areas a quick wipe-down.

Friday: The Infamous Toilet Brush

🕐 20 minutes

Let's face it: the toilet brush is a necessary evil. Every once in a while you really need to get in there and give the bowl a good scrub. The problem is that this is a nasty chore, and it's performed with a nasty implement. Not only does the toilet brush get gross pretty quickly, it's also hard to find a place to store it where it won't be in the way or attract attention. Check out your toilet brush. If it's discolored, damaged, or clogged with hair and grime, throw it out. Go to the store and check out the options, which include brushes with disposable heads that you can flush, making your job that much easier.

Almost Perfect

Save yourself some scrubbing right from the get go. You know those little blue cleaning tabs that go in the toilet tank? Use them! They keep your toilet cleaner for longer periods of time, make cleaning your toilet easier, and their clean smell helps freshen your bathroom.

Saturday: Organize the Bathroom for Multiple Users

🕐 30 minutes

If you have roommates, children, or other family members living with you and you're all sharing one bathroom, you have to find a way to store everyone's toiletries without clutter getting out of hand. One way to do this is to give each person his or her own shelf in a cabinet. For kids, make sure the cabinet is low enough for them to reach, and consider labeling each shelf with the child's name to give him or her a sense of ownership. If you have roommates, you might purchase a cart with various drawers, one for each of you, or mount cubbies on the wall. Make sure there are enough hooks or wall-mounted bars for everyone's towels, and encourage everyone to take their personal items (like robes, slippers, books, or music players) out of the bathroom when they're done.

Sunday: Summon Your Inner Artist

🕐 60 minutes

You've worked hard on your bathroom; now it's time to have some fun! Find a small project you can do as one of the final touches. For example, repaint a drab or peeling cabinet. Pick out a bright, cheerful color at the hardware store (making sure to splurge on mildew-resistant paint), and give that cabinet a fresh look. If you feel especially motivated, you can also refinish your tub using a specialty bathtub refinishing paint that you can find at your local hardware store. A brand spanking new tub will brighten up your bathroom instantaneously. Whatever you decide to do, go all out on your little project! It's the perfect way to put your personal stamp on the space and remind yourself that the bathroom is a part of your home, too.

Monday: Keep Travel-Size Toiletries Someplace Special

🕐 10 minutes

Travel-size toiletries definitely belong in your bathroom, but it makes sense to keep them separate from your other bathroom items. An easy way to do this is to designate a bag or a basket specifically for travel items. This way when you're packing for a trip you can easily pull out those adorable little toothpastes and shaving creams that you bought specifically for this purpose. If you're flying to your vacation destination, be sure to check the updated airline regulations online to see what you can carry on board and what needs to be kept in checked baggage. The last thing you want is to get pulled out of the security line to have your bag searched.

Tuesday: Move Your Toothbrush

🕐 5 minutes

Many bathrooms have a toothbrush holder built right into the wall above the sink. While this may seem like a handy thing, it actually might be doing more harm than good. Modern toothbrush designs have thicker handles, which often don't fit in standard-sized toothbrush holder holes. This causes brushes to stick up too high and lean at a funny angle. Also, storing your toothbrush out in the open like this leaves it susceptible to floating germs or to being knocked onto the floor by accident. Instead, keep your familys' toothbrushes in a cup inside the medicine cabinet where they'll be safe and out of the way.

Don't throw your old toothbrushes away; instead, use them to clean small, hard-to-reach areas around your home. A quick scrub at your grates and drains and around dirty faucets will give these dental duds a second life.

Wednesday: Declare Dental Territory

🕐 10 minutes

Like everything else in your bathroom, your dental products (toothpaste, floss, mouthwash) need their own spot. Instead of keeping all these items scattered around your bathroom, choose one area—a single shelf in a cabinet, for example—where dental items will reside. The easier it is to locate these products, the more likely you'll be to establish and stick with a daily dental routine. The next time your dentist congratulates you on a cavity-free visit, you can tell her that it was all due to home organization.

Thursday: Let That Loofah Go

🕐 5 minutes

Loofahs, shower puffs, and back scrubbers may seem like luxurious bath items, but they can quickly fall into a state of nastiness when kept in a damp bathroom. If any of your puffy, scrubby shower items are growing mold or getting clogged with soap scum, just throw them away. You can easily replace them or, better yet, switch to bar soap or a foaming body wash that doesn't require an application device. The fewer items you have in your shower, the better. Not only will this make cleaning easier, but you'll also have less opportunity for mold and mildew to collect in the first place.

Friday: Avoid Hand Towel Pitfalls

🕐 5 minutes

Don't you hate when you use the bathroom in someone else's house and find a dirty hand towel hung next to the sink? Or worse, no hand towel to speak of? You're left to search the bathroom for another towel and to hope you're not using someone's shower towel to dry your hands. You deserve better than this—and so do your guests—so be sure you give it to them. Always keep a clean hand towel hung near the sink, as well as a full bottle of hand soap. When the sink area is well stocked and maintained, your guests and family alike won't have to go looking elsewhere for what they need. It only takes a few minutes to do things right!

Saturday: Make Your Toilet Shine

🕐 5 minutes

What's worse than ring around the collar? Ring around the toilet. You know the ring we're talking about: that nasty brown stain inside your toilet bowl that won't completely disappear no matter how hard you scrub. Instead of trying to scrub the stain away, just pour a half cup bleach into the toilet bowl and let it sit for twenty minutes or overnight. When you flush, the ring should disappear. If that doesn't work, drop two Alka-Seltzer tablets into the bowl. The bubbles will help dislodge any grime and remove the stains. As a last-ditch effort, try a product called Lime Away. Some of the most stubborn stains in bathrooms are caused by lime buildup. This product should take care of the problem.

Sunday: Clean the Seat

While we're on the subject of the toilet, consider another area that often gets overlooked in a bathroom: the toilet seat. Most people stay on top of cleaning the toilet bowl, but they commonly forget about the seat. As the place where you sit your bare behind down, this surface is especially important to keep clean. The easiest way to do it is with flushable disinfecting bathroom wipes. Keep a container of these in a nearby cabinet and wipe down the toilet seat a few times a week. Most of these wipes are soaked with alcohol-based cleaners, so the wetness should evaporate almost immediately.

Almost Perfect

If you have company coming and don't have time to give your bathroom a thorough scrub, just Windex the mirrors and the top of the sink. Give your toilet a quick scrub and you'll be good to go!

22 JUST CLEAN ENOUGH

THE KITCHEN CALLS

Stand mixer. Coffee maker. Athletic equipment? Sound familiar? Yes, the kitchen tends to be a gathering place in the house. Great! You want to be able to socialize. But you don't want it to turn into a storage locker, home office, or a playroom. What to do with all that crap currently piled up on your counters? Get it out of there! You want a clean, organized, beautiful kitchen, so roll up your sleeves and get down to business.

Monday: Clear Off Those Counters

🕐 **20 minutes**

Believe it or not, your kitchen is not actually the best place for your laptop, your son's backpack, last week's newspaper, the unfolded laundry, or that birthday gift for your niece that you haven't gotten a chance to mail yet. Assess the items on your counters. Do all of them belong there? Remove those that don't and evaluate those that remain. Are there small appliances on your counters that you don't use often? Tuck them away in a cabinet or give them to someone who will use them. To free up counter space, utilize a paper-towel rack that hangs on the wall and consider appliances (such as a microwave) that can be installed under your cabinets.

Almost Perfect

Get rid of any appliances that only do one thing. Do you really need a sandwich maker *and* a George Foreman grill? An excess of appliances only makes your kitchen look more cluttered and takes up precious counter space.

Tuesday: Take Out the Trash

🕐 **10 minutes**

Is your trashcan working for you? This may sound like a ridiculous question, but one of the most common problem areas of the kitchen is the trash. Take a look at your trashcan. If it's broken, missing its lid, or just not meeting your needs, kick it to the curb and get a new one. Trashcans with lids are ideal for keeping bad smells in and pets out, and a can with a foot pedal keeps your hands free from bacteria when throwing things away. Once you have a trashcan that meets your needs, take care of it. Clean it and spray it with disinfectant on a regular basis.

Wednesday: Dish Rack Duty

🕐 5 minutes

If you do your dishes by hand, you probably have a dish rack next to your sink. This is fine, but if your dish rack has been taken over by yucky stains and buildup, throw it out and get a new one. Going forward, clean your dish rack regularly and put away your dishes as soon as they're dry. If you leave them sitting there, other members of your household will just pile theirs on top, and before you know it you'll have a leaning tower of plates—and an ideal climate for mold and bacteria—on your hands.

Thursday: What's under the Kitchen Sink?

🕐 20 minutes

Most likely the cabinet under your kitchen sink is brimming with household cleaners. Open up this cabinet and go through the items one by one. Separate those that you use on a regular basis from those that you never use or can't identify. Don't pour these cleaners down the drain or throw them in the trash; they may be toxic. Contact your local environmental agency or government office to find out how to dispose of these items safely. Once you've whittled your cleaners down to the necessities, wipe out the cabinet and replace them in an orderly fashion. Consider investing in adjustable-height shelving that slides out along rails and is specially designed to fit around awkward drainpipes.

Friday: Keep Spices Looking Nice

🕐 15 minutes

The spice rack or cabinet is typically a war zone. But take heart! There are a few different solutions to this problem. If you keep your spices in a cabinet, consider investing in a lazy Susan. The turntable action of this device offers 360-degree access to stored items. You could also buy a wall-mounted spice rack and hang it near your stove or another area where you prepare food. Then your spices will be right at your fingertips. You can also get small canisters that have magnets on the back so you can store items on your refrigerator. If your fridge is near your cooking area, this might be the perfect spice solution for you.

Saturday: Make a Mess

🕐 40 minutes

Ever heard the expression, "It has to get worse before it gets better"? This applies perfectly to the task at hand. Before you can organize your kitchen, you have to pull it apart and see what's there. That means emptying all cabinets and sorting through items one at a time. To begin, pull everything out of a single cabinet and take a look at the contents. What do you need and what can you get rid of? As you reduce the bulk in each cabinet, you'll find that it will be much easier to keep it clean.

Sunday: Just Say No to Junk

🕒 20 minutes

Ever heard the term junk drawer? Chances are you have at least one in your kitchen. When going through these, take on the role of a drill sergeant. Inspect each item and be merciless. Any chipped, broken, or outdated items go straight into the trash. If you find yourself hemming and hawing over something, throw it out. Ask yourself when you last used your strawberry huller, apple corer, or hard-boiled-egg slicer. If you can't remember, you have your answer. And don't hang onto things because you just might need them one day. Anything that's outlived its usefulness in your home might just find a purpose in someone else's.

Kitchen Week 2

Monday: Pay the Fridge a Visit

🕒 30 minutes

Ah, the refrigerator. You've probably been avoiding this one. Spoiled food, old, sticky spills . . . who wants to dive into that? Whether you want to or not, this task is a must. The first step in organizing your refrigerator is to empty it out and clean it, but you can do this a little at a time. Remove all the items from one shelf and wipe it down. Once that's done, start sorting.

Throw away anything that's expired or questionable and let go of items that you know you'll never eat. Next, take inventory of the items that remain and decide how you'll organize them. Keep similar items together. Take full advantage of the drawers, shelves, and refrigerator door.

Tuesday: Get Rid of Lingering Smells

🕒 5 minutes

Even if your fridge is white-glove clean (and let's be honest here, it probably isn't), it may still smell a little. It makes sense, though, right? Think of everything you keep in your fridge: fish, yesterday's takeout, burritos, cat food, curry, cheese, and plenty of items that are just waiting for next week's trash day, like just-past-its-expiration-date milk, fruit, and so on. You name it . . . it's stored in your fridge. An easy way to solve this problem is to stick an open container or box of baking soda in the back of your fridge. The baking soda will suck up the majority of smells and keep your fridge smelling like a dream—or a just-clean-enough fridge as the case may be.

Wednesday: Control Your Cutlery

🕒 15 minutes

If you're like most people, you probably have a cutlery drawer that is brimming with more than just cutlery. Perhaps you've got a few rubber bands, some plastic baggies, a box of tooth-picks, a set of corncob holders, and a bundle of twist ties. Sound familiar? Here's what you do: Remove everything from the drawer that is not a fork, knife, or spoon. If you don't already have one, buy yourself a cutlery holder to help keep the drawer organized. Also, make sure you have the right number of pieces of cutlery for your situation. If you have a family of seven, you're going to need more than three forks. If you live alone, you probably don't need sixteen spoons. Take out any extras and donate them. You'll be much happier when you can open that drawer and see exactly what you need.

Thursday: Relocate Fruit to the Fridge

🕐 5 minutes

A bowl of fresh fruit can look lovely on a counter or tabletop, but if you have a small kitchen, it might also be contributing to a cluttered look. If this is the case in your kitchen, con-sider moving your fresh fruit to the refrigerator. But before you do so, check the ripeness. Most fruits, like lemons, oranges, apples, and grapes, do not continue to ripen after they've been picked, so they'll do best in your refrigerator. In fact, they will stay fresher longer in the fridge, especially in the hot summer months. However, fruits like mangos and nectarines will con-tinue to ripen in your fruit bowl on the counter, so if they're harder than you'd like when you buy them, leave them out for a few days before transferring them to the fridge. And finally, never put bananas in the refrigerator as they will turn brown in no time.

Friday: Try Nesting

🕐 10 minutes

This is not a recommendation that you have a child in order to get your kitchen organized; that would actually be counterproductive. We're talking about kitchen items that come in various sizes that can be stacked and stored together—taking up less space. Nesting mixing bowls are great for various tasks. Use the smallest bowl to beat an egg, the medium-sized bowl to prepare a fruit salad, and the largest bowl to mix up a big batch of cookie dough. Drinking glasses that fit inside one another will take up less space in your cabinet, and nesting measuring cups will only need a corner of a drawer. So if you have nesting items already, make sure they are being stored together. If you don't have these, consider replacing older items with these space savers.

Saturday: Bring Order to Your Brooms and Mops

🕐 10 minutes

Brooms, mops, dusters, and similar items can be tough to place in the home. Many people keep them in the kitchen, but they're not that pretty to look at so you don't want them out in the open. What you need is a tall, narrow space where these will be accessible but still out of the way. This might be a corner of your food pantry or the sliver of space between your fridge and the wall. Wherever you choose to stash these items, be sure that you keep them neat and tidy. Don't hang on to ratty old brooms and mops that are past their prime. A hair-clogged broom or filthy mop head will only transfer hair, dust, and dirt back onto your floors.

Sunday: Clear Off Tops of Cabinets

🕐 30 minutes

While you may think no one really notices, all that stuff you store on top of your cabinets gives your kitchen a cluttered, messy look. See if you can relocate some of those items to places that are out of sight. Your kitchen will look cleaner and more spacious this way. If you absolutely need to utilize the space on top of your cabinets for storage, pick up some attractive baskets or bins that complement the existing décor. That way, you can store items in a neat and organized fashion that won't detract from the overall look of the room.

Almost Perfect

If you have kids, you're likely afraid to use good dishes, but as an adult you don't want to be eating off plastic for years. Invest in some unbreakable glasses and dishes that look good, and store your nice china somewhere until it's safe to put it back into everyday use.

Monday: Evaluate Your Oven Mitts

🕐 10 minutes

What's the current oven mitt situation in your kitchen? Do you have too many and have trouble finding a place to put them all? You only need two oven mitts (because you only have two hands) and maybe three or four potholders in your kitchen. More than that are unnecessary and will take up space needed for other things. Are your oven mitts and potholders old, burned, torn, or otherwise ineffectual? Make sure these items are of high quality and are thick enough so you don't feel any heat coming through them. The minute one of these pops a hole, throw it out. A third-degree burn will not help you in your reorganization efforts.

Tuesday: Start Composting

🕐 5 minutes

Banana peels, eggshells, coffee grounds, and other food scraps may seem like garbage, but they can actually have a second life as compost. If you're a gardener, decomposed food scraps can provide rich nutrients to your soil. Instead of scraping off your plates into the trashcan or garbage disposal, put fruit and vegetable scraps into an airtight jug. As these items slowly decompose, add them to your soil for the health of your plants. You can also buy small, discreet countertop compost pails at many home stores. These items make it easy to gather food waste indoors while keeping odors to a minimum. You can store a compost pail under the sink, on the counter, or in a cabinet for accessibility.

Wednesday: Reduce, Reuse, Recycle

🕐 15 minutes

Yes, recycling is important, but so is a system that works for you—and having recyclables stacked willy-nilly in your kitchen isn't it. Instead, purchase a recycling sorter with at least two different bins: one for plastic and glass, one for paper products. Keep in mind, however, that, like trash, even well-rinsed bottles and cans will create a sticky, stinky residue in your bin. Wash it frequently to keep your kitchen smelling fresh.

Thursday: Create a Family Message Center

🕐 20 minutes

If you share your household with other people, chances are you all have very different schedules that are hard to coordinate. To make things easier—and to avoid accumulating piles of calendars and to-do lists—create a family message center in the kitchen. This message center may include a large corkboard or dry-erase board for posting messages and slots for sorting mail. You can also maintain a food-shopping list that all members of the family can contribute to. Everyone in the family will know to check the message board so that even when schedules conflict, you and your family members can communicate about upcoming events and household chores.

Friday: Establish a Coupon System

🕐 20 minutes

How would you like to save $5, $10, or even $20 every time you shop for groceries? If this sounds appealing, coupon clipping may be for you. Searching for and clipping coupons from the newspaper or from advertising circulars can be a time-consuming task, but many people enjoy it as a relaxing rainy-day activity. Use a binder with clear pockets to sort, categorize, and store your coupons. For example, you may have categories called Cleaning Products and Pet Care Products, and you simply place all related coupons in that category within the same pocket. An alternative is to use a small file box and store your coupons alphabetically, either by product name or brand name. As a general rule, clip and store coupons for only those products you already use or definitely want to try. If you're not careful, your coupon file could easily get cluttered with coupons you have no intention of using.

Almost Perfect

Put silicon oven liners in your oven. You can take these out and throw them in your dishwasher and avoid hours of scrubbing. You can also buy silicon drawer liners. Put them in and when you clean out the drawer, throw them in the dishwasher, too!

Saturday: Round Up Your Recipes

🕐 20 minutes

If you enjoy cooking, chances are you've acquired many recipes in many different forms—from cookbooks and magazine clippings to printouts from the Internet and handwritten notes from friends and family. Instead of shoving crumpled pieces of paper in all available nooks and crannies and struggling to find the recipe you want when you want it, pick up a three-ring binder with dividers along with a bunch of clear plastic sleeves that you can insert papers into. Divide the binder into sections, such as Appetizers, Chicken Dishes, Desserts, and so on, and then file your recipes within the binder. Keep it with your cookbooks, on a shelf in the kitchen. An alternative is to file your recipes in a file cabinet or recipe box.

Sunday: Take a Look at Lighting

🕐 30 minutes

The way that you light your kitchen will have a dramatic effect on how you work and feel in that space. Oftentimes kitchens have harsh overhead lights that glare on all who enter. Ideally, you'll have a few different types of lighting so that you can alternate them depending on your needs and the time of day. Invest in lighting that you love—lamps can work in a kitchen, as can beam or spot lights that will give you soft, steady light in exactly the place where you need it. Soft, ample light can increase your efficiency, improve your mood, and transform your kitchen into a place of peace and hospitality.

Kitchen Week 4

Monday: Pare Down Plastics

🕐 20 minutes

A familiar slapstick scene played out in kitchens far and wide is opening a cabinet door and being awash in a shower of tubs and lids. Don't let this happen to you! First, buy plastic containers in a single shape. Go for square or round, but don't have both. Mismatched shapes will take up extra cabinet space and prevent you from stacking to the max. Mount a separate rack for lids inside the cabinet door and your shelves will look department-store neat. Also, are you still squirreling away the plastic tubs and containers from cottage cheese, margarine, and Chinese takeout? Do you really need to save every last one of them? Instead, recycle them or donate them to a school art class.

Tuesday: Hang It Up!

⏱ 20 minutes

Are you running low on cabinet space but have some good-looking pots and pans or mugs that you wouldn't mind putting on display? Overhead pot racks suspended from the ceiling are a creative use of air space. Make sure the rack is securely bolted in place and up to the task of handling a heavy weight load. Hanging pot racks run the gamut of styles, from ornate iron-work to thin minimalist wooden strips, to match just about any décor. Some have built-in shelves for lids or additional display storage. You can also install a few hooks underneath a cabinet to hang attractive mugs or teacups. This will free up some cabinet space while adding a homey touch to the look of the room.

Wednesday: Attention, Magnet Maniacs!

⏱ 15 minutes

In many homes, the refrigerator winds up becoming a giant, messy canvas for magnet collages. While it's nice to have the phone number of your favorite pizza delivery service handy, and it's easy to tack up all the photos of your nieces and nephews you get in holiday cards, you can put the refrigerator's magnetic properties to better use. Instead, make your magnets into a work of art. Buy a magnetic board and install it on a wall in your kitchen. Display magnets from trips you've taken or choose a few of your favorite photos and put them in magnetic frames. Just don't go overboard.

Thursday: Find a Place for Pesky Plastic Bags

🕐 15 minutes

From grocery bags to the bags the newspaper comes in, plastic bags are everywhere. While they are useful to hang on to, things can quickly get out of hand. Instead of just shoving them in the cabinet under the kitchen sink or stuffing them into a drawer, come up with a system that saves space by making the bags as compact as possible. For instance, pick up a plastic bag holder that can be mounted on the inside of a cabinet door, or a hanging sleeve that can go in a pantry or closet. Load bags into the top of the device, pressing down in order to remove all the air, and then, when you need a bag, just pull one from the bottom.

Friday: Filter Water at the Source

🕐 20 minutes

If you're someone who doesn't like to drink water straight from the tap, you may be the proud owner of one of those large, plastic filtering jugs. While it's nice to have cold, filtered water at the ready, this device takes up a lot of space in your fridge or on your countertop. An alternative is a filtering fixture that can be installed right on your kitchen faucet. Most of these fixtures have on and off settings or can simply be moved aside when you're just washing dishes and don't need filtered water. This device does have a filter that will need to be changed every so often, but overall it will save some precious space and make your kitchen a little less cluttered.

Almost Perfect

When cooking, clean as you go. Rinse out bowls and put them right in your dishwasher, and wipe down the cutting board when you're done with it. This way, you don't have to go back and clean when you'd rather be enjoying your meal and time with your family.

Saturday: Do Some Drawer and Cabinet Maintenance

🕐 40 minutes

Take a tour of your kitchen. Are there any drawers with missing pulls or wheels that have come off the track? Are there any cabinets with creaky hinges or doors that don't close all the way? If you have missing or damaged drawer pulls, take this opportunity to choose a new design and replace them all. For creaky hinges, apply some household lubricant and open and close the cabinet door two or three times to help it circulate. If you find a cabinet door that always hangs open just slightly, pick up a cabinet magnet kit. Simply affix one magnet to the surface of the open cabinet and the other to the inside of the cabinet door. When you close the door, they should meet and attract, keeping the door closed.

Sunday: Get a Knife Makeover

🕐 20 minutes

What kind of shape are your knives in? Are the blades dull and the handles loose? Dull blades require you to put in twice the effort, and loose handles can cause you to slip and cut yourself. While you don't need more stuff on your kitchen countertop, there is one item that is worth the several square inches it takes up: a knife block. Essentially, it's just a block of wood with slits of different sizes for all your different size knives: the chopping knife, the bread knife, the paring knife, and so on. Some knife blocks also come with a sharpener so you can sharpen your own knives at home. Others include slots for kitchen shears and other handy tools. If counter space is seriously at a premium, another option is a wall-mounted magnetic knife strip.

Kitchen Week 5

Monday: Liner Note

🕐 20 minutes

Drawers and cabinets looking a little drab? Give them a pick-me-up by inserting some drawer and shelf liners. These are easy-to-clean plastic liners with adhesive backing that come in lots of pretty patterns. Before you scoff, consider how these liners can change your life. Not only do they serve to protect your drawers and cabinetry (a big concern, to be sure), they also kick the aesthetic appeal up a notch. You can even get liners in scented varieties, adding another sensory dimension to the experience of looking for a measuring cup. And goodness knows, the hunt for a measuring cup should be a stimulating one.

Tuesday: It's a Bird. It's a Plane. It's a Grapefruit!

🕐 15 minutes

By now, you should be storing most of your fruit in the fridge (see "Relocate Fruit to the Fridge"), but there may be some stragglers (bananas, ripening apricots, plums, and so on) that you don't know what to do with. Pick up a handy-dandy hanging basket set, which gets fruits and veggies up off the counter and into the air. Most hanging baskets have two or three tiers; you can devote one to fruits, one to vegetables, and one to the special items that don't play well with others. For example, bananas emit ethylene, a gas that causes other fruit to ripen at an increased rate. And garlic can transfer its strong smell to other fruits and vegetables it's hanging out with. Keep these separate from the group, and everyone will be happier.

Wednesday: You Stink, Microwave

🕐 5 minutes

Got a smelly microwave with splatters and smears of food as decoration? Time to do something about it. Fill a microwave-able bowl three-quarters of the way with water and add ¼ cup lemon juice to the bowl. Put the bowl with the water-lemon juice mixture into the microwave and run it on high for one minute. When it beeps, remove the bowl and wipe out the microwave using a damp rag or sponge and the condensation that has formed from the lemon water. And there you have it: a nice, clean microwave that smells lemony fresh!

Thursday: Buy a Breadbox

🕐 10 minutes

If you're like most families, you don't really know what to do with all the bread you buy. Maybe it's tossed on the top of your fridge or piled up on your counter. Solve this problem by heading to your local Ikea (or Target, or anywhere you can buy kitchen items) and pick up a breadbox. Gather all your loaves, rolls, and muffins together and put them in their new, crumb-free home. As a bonus, you now have a visual for all those times when someone asks you if an item is "bigger than a breadbox."

Friday: Control Coffeemaker Chaos

🕐 10 minutes

Coffee is delicious, and the caffeine sure does come in handy, but is all this really necessary? You have a French press on the counter, a drip coffeemaker on the table, and a moka pot on the stovetop. There's also a bag of coffee beans, a grinder, a package of filters, a strainer . . . the list goes on forever. To simplify, choose your favorite style of coffee and get rid of the rest. Give the extraneous machinery and coffee to a good cause, such as your coworker who oversleeps and arrives late to work every day. Both your kitchen—and your coworker—will thank you.

Saturday: Got Stovetop Splatters?

🕐 30 minutes

There are two ways to clean a stovetop: the hard way and the easy way. The hard way involves rubber gloves and scrubber sponges and elbow grease. Sounds fun, right? Not so much. To that end, we're going to keep it simple and just talk about the easy way to get rid of that caked-on stovetop gunk. Simply spray the surface with an all-purpose kitchen cleaner, such as Formula 409, and let it sit for about twenty minutes. Then take a damp sponge and wipe up the splatters, which should have softened for easy cleanup. Also make sure you clean the area around the burners. If it's a gas stove, remove the burner plates and soak them in hot, soapy water while you let the all-purpose cleaner do its work on the stovetop. When you come back, just rinse the burner plates, wipe off the stovetop, and you're ready to go do something a lot more fun.

Sunday: Create a Cooking Station

🕐 **10 minutes**

If you cook at home a lot, you probably have a few spices, oils, or other staples that you use in most of your recipes. A great way to prevent unnecessary trips to the cabinet and to make cooking easier is to set up a little station right next to your stove. A great tool to use is a desktop organizer, which has lots of slots and sections for a variety of different-sized items. For example, you might keep a set of salt and pepper shakers in the notepad holder, a small bottle of olive oil where the Wite-Out would go, and a couple of mixing utensils in the pen cup. Many of these desktop organizers are on turntables for easy access to all the products therein.

WHERE SHALL WE DINE?

The dining room is a bit of a chameleon. Typically it operates as a space for dining, meeting, homework, and any number of other tasks. The reason? Well, the table, for starters. The dining room table is a catchall for newspapers, takeout menus, bills . . . anything that doesn't have a home somewhere else. But in order to get the most out of this room, you need to lay some ground rules—and stick to them. Follow the quick tips in this chapter and you'll have your dining room back in no time.

Monday: First Things First: The Table

🕐 15 minutes

All you're going to do today is excavate your dining room table. Think of it as an archaeological dig. Sort through all the items and determine which belong in the room and which do not. Old newspapers and magazines? Recycle them. Your daughter's math textbook? Bring it to her bedroom. A mug half full with three-day-old coffee? Put it in the kitchen sink, for goodness sake! Once the dining room table is cleared of all its clutter you can begin to consider what the table—and the room—should really be used for. Will you eat most of your meals here? Will the kids use it for their homework? Will you host your weekly poker party? Make a list of all the potential uses for this room.

Tuesday: Care for Your Chairs

🕐 20 minutes

If the table is the most important part of the dining room, then the chairs are the runners-up. Take a look at your dining room chairs. Are they in good shape? Do they all match? Is the upholstery stained or torn or broken? In many ways your dining room is a showpiece. It's where you entertain your guests and where you enjoy your meals as a family. The chairs that go around the dining room table need to be sturdy, well-built, and comfortable, not to mention attractive. While fixing a chair leg or recovering a seat might seem like a small improvement, it could make all the difference in your dining experience and the look and feel of the room.

Almost Perfect

Want to reupholster your dining room chairs but can't afford to have someone do it for you? Do it yourself! Remove the seat from one of your chairs (it might be screwed on, but in some cases, it will just pop off) and bring it to your local fabric store. Tell a staff member what you're planning to do and ask for help choosing and measuring fabric and/or cushioning. Chances are, they'll even be able to give you some helpful tips on how to do the job.

Wednesday: Bring in Some Baskets

🕒 15 minutes

If you've elected to use the dining room as a homework space for the kids and a place where you can pay bills and catch up on paperwork, invest in some wicker or metal-mesh baskets to keep papers in order. If you have one for each of your kids, they'll feel a sense of ownership and are more likely to keep their items tidy. As for you, designate a basket for bills to be paid, one for mail to go out, and so on. Instead of keeping these on the table, make sure these baskets have a home. Keep them hidden in a cabinet, or, if they're neat and attractive, consider placing them on a sideboard or other piece of furniture.

Thursday: Make It Pretty

🕒 10 minutes

Beauty and order are closely related; if your dining room table looks nice and neat, your family is much less likely to cover it in clutter. Put out a bowl of fresh seasonal fruits or a nice tablecloth. Bring in flowers from your garden and arrange them as a centerpiece. These items can serve as a reminder that your dining table should stay as clean and attractive as possible. After all, when you seek to make different corners of your home beautiful, you are all the more likely to feel energized about keeping them orderly.

Friday: Utilize Existing Storage Space

🕐 **15 minutes**

Perhaps your dining area has built-in storage or a stand-alone storage piece. This storage can be useful if you are discriminating about the items you place there. Not only can you keep fine china separate from your everyday dishes, but you can also keep part of this storage empty so that you have a place to stow papers and other items when company is coming. If your cabinet has glass doors, your china will be protected as you show off the beauty of your pieces. If your fine china will be stored in drawers or closed cabinets, however, you'll want to take steps to properly protect these expensive and fragile items. Use quilted vinyl cases for china to keep dust away and to prevent chipping and scratching.

Saturday: Make a List

🕐 **10 minutes**

Sit down with a pen and a piece of paper and make a list with two columns. Column A is for the things you like about your dining room, and Column B is for the things you don't like so much. Take your time with this list, and consider every little detail, from the rug on the floor to the lighting on the ceiling. Once you've established what you like about the room, you can work from there, adding complementary elements and removing things that detract from the room's overall appearance.

Sunday: Clean Up Your Flatware

🕐 20 minutes

Why wait for a special occasion to use your nice things. Make tonight special (Sunday dinner anyone!) by using your family silver. While sterling silver is beautiful, it tarnishes over time, so take some time to clean it up. There are many different metal polishes on the market. Some polishes can be corrosive, so take care to follow the manufacturer's instructions. When washing your fine flatware after a meal, use only warm, sudsy water. Avoid using harsh dishwashing detergents that contain chlorides. Also, avoid lemon-scented detergents, which contain acids that may harm the metal. It's also important to hand-dry silver, especially knife blades, to avoid spotting and pitting. If you'll be washing both silver and stainless-steel flatware in the dishwasher, don't put them in the same basket section. You want to avoid allowing one metal to touch the other.

Dining Room Week 2

Monday: Install Mood Lighting

🕐 20 minutes

A change in lighting doesn't have to cost you much, but it can dramatically transform the way a space feels. If you're planning to work and entertain in this space, you might want to invest in at least a few different types of lighting. For above the table, there are benefits to a chandelier. Soft lighting is much better in this space than harsh overhead lights. If the light shines up toward the ceiling and then reflects back down on you and your guests, this will be more flattering than a straight-down beam. Typically, when you're hosting a formal or romantic dinner, you'll want mood lighting. You may want to consider installing a lighting fixture with lights that can be dimmed.

Tuesday: Dewax Your Candlesticks

🕐 **10 minutes**

Don't you hate how wax gets all over your candlesticks every time you burn candles? Then, when you try to scrape it off, a filmy residue is left behind. To remove wax from a candlestick made of silver or another metal, put it in the freezer until the wax is hardened and then use a plastic spatula to scrape it off. If there are any remaining bits, melt them away by pouring boiling water over the candlestick or by submerging it in a tub of boiling water.

Wednesday: Set Up Your Liquor Cabinet

🕐 **5 minutes**

Take it easy, this step is not about fixing yourself a drink—but you can have one if you think it will help. Whether you have a stand-alone liquor cabinet or a wine rack built into your buffet or credenza, keep all of your related supplies together in one area. In addition to the actual bottles of wine and liquor, some of the supplies you'll want to move to your liquor cabinet include a bottle opener, bottle stoppers, cocktail napkins, cocktail shaker, corkscrew, decanter, foil cutter, ice bucket, pitcher, wine glasses, shot glasses, and a bartender's mixing guide.

Some wine racks have special shelves or cabinets to store these accessories.

Thursday: Stop Wine-ing

🕐 15 minutes

Picture your wine cabinet: an organized drawer filled with wine accessories (see "Set Up Your Liquor Cabinet"), several rows of your favorite vintage (or cheap $10 wine . . . who are we to judge), hanging wine glasses . . . and dust. Lots of it. "Not me you say!" But, if your wine cabinet doesn't have a glass front (and even if it does), it's time to take a closer look. Be honest, your wine glasses—especially the ones in the back—and bottles are coated in a thin layer of gross. Run your wine glasses through the dishwasher; remember to put them on the top shelf to keep the stems safe. Then take each bottle out and give it a good wipe-down. Now's a good time to take stock of what you have. Do you have wines that are just about to peak? Some that are past their prime? One you'd like to pop open right now? Dust down your wine cabinet before you put everything back in and sit back and enjoy.

Friday: Give the Kitchen a Break

🕐 15 minutes

If your kitchen is packed to the gills but your dining room is spacious and empty, give a few kitchen items a new place to dwell. Consider relocating decorative mugs or bowls that you only use for special occasions, candlesticks for use on the dining room table, and flower vases and planters. The more attractive items can be out on display, while the others can be tucked away in a sideboard or hutch with doors. While this grand relocation is a solid plan, don't go overboard. Cleaning out your kitchen only to overload your dining room doesn't make sense. Be discerning about the items you choose to move, and only display those that will enhance the look of the room.

Saturday: Hang Paintings or Photographs

🕐 15 minutes

This is a dining room, and therefore the emphasis is on the dining—the table, the china, and all the other related accoutrements. But while you don't want to clutter up the space with too much decoration, blank walls aren't appealing either. Look around for pieces that you think would work in your dining room. You might choose something food related, such as a few brightly colored paintings of fruit or a series of photographs taken in restaurants. If you have a friend or family member who's an artist or photographer, commission that person to create a few unique pieces for the room. This is an easy way to add some style as well as a personal touch.

Sunday: Clean Your Chandelier

🕐 20 minutes

There is nothing less appealing—or appetizing—than a dust-covered chandelier hanging right over your head during dinner. To do a quick clean before company arrives, run a duster over the chandelier. Just be sure to wipe down the table afterward. To thoroughly clean the crystals, just remove them from the chandelier and run them through the dishwasher. Be sure to use a gentle soap, not a harsh abrasive; after all, you're just removing dust, not last night's dinner.

Dining Room Week 3

Monday: Create a Centerpiece

🕐 20 minutes

Sorry to tell you this, but that pile of unpaid bills and unopened mail does not make a great centerpiece for your dining room table. Clear off that clutter and recruit the family into a creative effort. You can make a personalized centerpiece using a collage of small picture frames with family photos in them, or make a natural centerpiece using pretty stones, pinecones, and other items you find outside. Whenever you enter the dining room you'll be delighted to see your creation on the table instead of a mound of paperwork.

Tuesday: Give Cleaning Products the Heave-Ho!

🕐 5 minutes

If there's one category of items that doesn't belong in your dining room, it's cleaning products. Unfortunately, they seem to gravitate toward this particular room. Sure, it's easier to remember to dust if the oil soap and rag are sitting out on the table, but that's not going to help your clutter situation. The same goes for brooms, mops, and vacuum cleaners. All of these tools and products belong in a closet or pantry where you can easily access them without having to look at them all the time. If you're worried about being able to wipe up spills quickly, you can keep a roll of paper towels hidden in a cabinet somewhere, but that's it. It would be too ironic to have your cleaning supplies be the reason your home is a mess!

Wednesday: Move Extras into Storage

🕐 20 minutes

If you're someone who likes to have company over for dinner, you might have extra chairs, a leaf for your dining room table, and maybe even an extra folding table or two available for the evenings when you entertain. It's great that you're prepared, but you need to keep these items out of the dining room when they're not in use. As soon as the guests leave, disassemble them, fold them up, or do whatever you have to do to make them portable, and then get 'em out of there. Don't lean an extra table or folding chairs against a wall; that will only make the room look crowded and not finished. Instead, store these items in a closet, the laundry room, or the basement. It won't kill you to have to pull them out each time you're planning to have people over.

Thursday: Protect Your Table

🕐 10 minutes

Unfortunately, linens alone will not protect your table from spills, scratches, nicks, and burns, but table pads will help them out. A table pad is just what it sounds like: a pad that sits between your table and tablecloth. You can find them pretty much anywhere table linens are sold, or if you have a table that's an unusual size or shape, you can get them customized. These pads will greatly extend the life of your table—and will help you control your own panic when a hot item is set down on the table or a glass of wine spills.

Friday: No Pets, Please!

🕒 10 minutes

The command, "No Pets!," doesn't mean that your pet can't hang out in the dining room if she wants (good luck trying to stop her), but it does mean that her *things* should be elsewhere. This includes toys, food dishes and water bowls, beds, leashes, raincoats, and any other pet-related paraphernalia. Yes, you love your pets, but their stuff will only serve to clutter up what is supposed to be a clean and serene space. Choose an area of the house that will be your pet's "home," and then move all her belongings to that space.

Almost Perfect

If you have pets, get them groomed on a regular basis. The less fur they shed, the less you have to clean up! Also, if you wash them at home, let them dry off outside. The last thing you need in your clean house is a wet dog.

Saturday: Look Down

🕒 20 minutes

Look down at the floor. Are you standing on a rug? Hardwood? Linoleum? Does the room have wall-to-wall carpeting? Whatever you find there, ask yourself if the floor situation is what you want it to be. If you have a rug on the floor, check it for wear, stains, or damage that could be detracting from the look of the room. If you have hardwood or linoleum that has seen better days, maybe you want to put down carpet. Write down your ideas and do some research to find out prices of the options you're considering. Even though you may not act on your desire any time soon, visualizing the room looking the way you want can help you start moving in that direction.

Sunday: Pull an Idea Out of a Hat

🕐 **20 minutes**

Round up your family and tell them you need their help figuring out what to do in the dining room. Give each person a piece of paper (yourself included), and ask them to write down one idea for a way to make the dining room even better. Put a bowl in the middle of the table and have everyone fold up and throw in their idea. Then have everyone reach in and take someone else's idea, and go around the table reading the ideas out loud. Have a discussion. Brainstorm. Chances are, with your heads put together, you'll come up with the perfect finishing touch for the room. And, without even realizing it, you'll be using this room for its intended purpose: quality time with your family.

Dining Room Week 4

Monday: Get Your Shine On

🕐 **10 minutes**

In the dining room, it's all about the furniture: the table and chairs, the china cabinet, the sideboard . . . all those pieces that you're keeping clutter free, right? These are the parts of the room that the activity revolves around, and you want to keep them looking their best. If you have wood furniture in your dining room—or anywhere else in your house for that matter—give it a polish every once in a while using a product made specifically for that purpose, such as Liquid Gold; it's expensive, but well worth it. And if you use the same rag every time, the Liquid Gold will get soaked in, making it easy to just run the rag over you woodwork before company arrives. Or make your own wood polish at home. Mix two parts vegetable or olive oil and one part lemon juice in a medium-sized bowl. Dip a clean, lint-free cloth into the mixture and rub the wood in the direction of the grain. Then rub with a clean, dry cloth until the wood shines.

Almost Perfect

Keep a bag of rags on hand and wash them once a week. Use these to shine, dust, dry, wipe, and wash anything at hand. Not sure where to get rags? Buy them at the store or cut up old T-shirts that are torn, stained, or too old to wear or donate.

Tuesday: Go Green with Cloth Napkins

🕒 5 minutes

Do you have a special event coming up, such as a holiday dinner or an anniversary party? Do you just want to make every meal with your family special? Take dinner up a notch by foregoing paper napkins and using cloth ones instead. This will give your guests—and your kids—a sense of occasion, and you'll keep dozens of disposable napkins from winding up in the trash. Yes, you'll have to wash the cloth napkins when you're done with them, but use an energy-saver setting on your washing machine to save water and keep your electric bill low. Mother Nature will thank you.

Wednesday: Protect Your Placemats

🕐 5 minutes

Placemats help keep your dining room table free of food stains, and they come in all sorts of different designs and materials. Placemats are especially great if you have kids; you can get them with fun, colorful prints and educational information printed on them. But as awesome as placemats are, people tend to get lazy about them. Maybe you leave them on the table all the time or forget to wipe up food and liquid stains between meals. If you're a placemat lover, act like it! Take care of the ones you have, or if it's time for replacements, go out and buy really beautiful ones that will enhance the look of your dining room. Also, make sure they're made of a durable, washable material so you can keep them looking great for years to come.

Thursday: Have a Designated Craft Cart

🕐 15 minutes

Do you sit at your dining room table to do scrapbooking or other projects? Do your kids use the table as a work surface for school assignments and crafts? If so, use a file cabinet or cart to store supplies and projects in progress. Cabinets and carts on wheels are especially nice as they can be easily retrieved and put away again. This way, you can have projects out and handy, but they won't be cluttering the table and you can store the cart in another room if it doesn't go with your dining room décor. You can also use this as a tool to teach your kids to clean up after craft time. If everyone works to keep the dining area clear, then everyone will be able to enjoy it.

Friday: Look Up

🕐 **5 minutes**

Sit down at your dining room table and look up. What do you see? Your ceiling? Your chandelier? Cobwebs? Unless it's Halloween (and even if it is), this is not a good look for your dining room. Grab your duster and give those high-up spaces a once-over, making sure to wipe out or shake free any bugs that are no longer with us—especially if they've been lingering in your lighting fixture. Pay special attention to the corners of the room. The dust that accumulates there will come away easily, leaving your former Halloween house clean and cobweb free.

Almost Perfect

Dust baseboards and corners with a duster that has a pole. You'll save time—and your back.

Saturday: Hide the Evidence

🕐 **15 minutes**

Got something ugly in your dining room, such as an air conditioner, radiator, or view into your neighbor's bathroom? Simply cover it up. Invest in a folding screen or room divider, which will add aesthetic value to the room while obscuring the offending eyesore. You can also buy radiator covers that do double duty: they'll cover up an ugly radiator and give you an extra shelf of storage space. You can also reorganize your room so the ugly thing is covered up by a tall piece of furniture. Don't spend a lot of money or time on this problem, though; chances are, there's a quick fix right under your nose already.

Sunday: Vacuuming Doesn't Have to Suck

🕐 10 minutes

A super quick, super easy way to spruce up your dining room is to go over the floor quickly with the vacuum. If you have a rug on the floor, start there. Move the chairs but not the table, and pay special attention to the areas where people walk and where crumbs might fall to the floor. As for the rest of the room, stick to the traffic areas; don't even think about moving the china cabinet! If there are dust bunnies back there, they're small and no one else is going to see them.

LIVING ROOM REDUX

The living room is perhaps the only area of the house without a defined purpose. You cook in the kitchen, you eat in the dining room, but you *live* in your living room, which can make it a breeding ground for clutter. Some use the space for watching TV; others use it for reading or playing games. But no matter how you're using your living room, it's time to organize it to fit your needs.

Monday: Take Stock

🕐 15 minutes

Take a good look around. What do you see? Papers from work? Those belong in your home office or in your briefcase or work bag someplace out of the way. Are your kids' toys strewn about? Either have your kids bring them to their rooms or, if you don't mind them being in the living room, think about an organizational system that could help keep them neat and put away. Is your couch hidden beneath piles of unfolded laundry? Relocate these to the laundry room or bedroom. Once you have the living room down to the items that belong there, you can begin to draw up a plan for the space.

Tuesday: Assign "Homes" to the Clutter

🕐 20 minutes

So much goes into the living room, yet many people do not have specific spots for all the clutter. If, for example, your children play in that room but all of their toys are still relegated to their bedrooms (with the expectation that they—or you—carry those items to their room every night), it might be easier to put a toy basket in the living room so putting toys away will be less of a challenge. If you like to read in this room but the newspapers and magazines tend to pile up on the coffee table, invest in a couple of baskets—one for paper products that are ready for the recycling bin and another for those publications that you're still reading. If books and DVDs don't have a place of their own, think about what kind of shelving unit could help keep them in order.

Wednesday: Rethink Your Furniture

🕐 20 minutes

Sit down with a pad of paper, a pen, and some furniture catalogs. Clarify the overall purpose and main functions of your living area, and then decide which of your current furniture pieces work for you and which don't. Also jot down a list of any pieces you're interested in adding, based on your needs. For furniture, less is more, so choose pieces that will be best utilized within the room. How about a coffee table or ottoman that opens up to reveal storage, or a sofa that contains a stowaway bed for guests? Once you've assessed what you have and what you need, flip through the catalogs and circle any items that you strike your fancy. Furniture can be a big investment, so make sure you think these decisions through before making any purchases.

Thursday: Entertain Yourself

🕐 30 minutes

If you keep your television and related items in your living room, take a look at how your entertainment system is arranged. If it's currently a jumbled mess of wires and boxes and manuals and remote controls, it's time to take charge. Start by taking inventory of all of the electronics you have: television, cable box, DVD player, stereo, video-game system, surround-sound system, speakers, and so on. Make sure everything is where it should be and roll up the wires. You don't need a nest hanging out behind your entertainment center. Be sure, too, that any furniture that will house electronics is well ventilated, as electronics produce a fair amount of heat.

Friday: Create Storage

🕐 20 minutes

Storage in the living area can be a tricky thing. First, determine what you need to store, and then be creative. For CDs, DVDs, and video games, you can purchase a display rack/organizer that holds your entire collection. This can be a freestanding unit, one that is mounted on a wall, or one that fits in your entertainment center. If it's a freestanding unit, you might place it in an unused corner of a room so that you can better utilize this space. You may also want to invest in a multifunctional universal remote control so that you can replace the separate remotes for your TV, cable box, and DVD player with one unit. An alternative is to place a remote-control caddy on the coffee table or near the TV to help you keep track of your different remotes.

Almost Perfect

Try a universal remote. Why have a separate remote for your TV, DVD player, and cable or satellite box when you can make due with just one?

Saturday: Organize Art and Collectibles

🕐 45 minutes

Displaying artwork, statues, trinkets, memorabilia, or collectibles can be tricky, especially in limited space. Go through your collection and throw away items that are broken or that you no longer want. Only display a few items that you really love. Don't be afraid of white space on the walls, either. It can give your eyes a welcome break from visual clutter and can make a room feel larger. When hanging pictures or artwork, try to keep them at eye level, and group them fairly close together. Make sure your collections or items are properly lit and that the display you create is visually appealing and lacks clutter.

Sunday: Spruce Up Your Home Library

🕐 60 minutes

To create a well-organized personal library, begin by sorting through your entire collection. Weed out books you no longer want—honestly, do you really need those old college textbooks?—and give them away to friends or donate them to a local library, thrift shop, or hospital. Keep in mind that books do not need to fill your entire bookcase. A little empty space provides a feeling of spaciousness and creates an opportunity for variety—and it leaves room for you to display some artwork or knickknacks. Also, by leaving some empty space in your bookshelf, you convey to yourself and your family that there is always room to grow.

Living Room Week 2

Monday: Make the Most of a Small Space

🕐 30 minutes

If you're challenged in the square-footage department, your living area may also double as your home office, guest room, or dining area. In this case, you want to utilize space to its utmost potential. Install a window seat with storage beneath it, or put cushions on top of a sturdy wooden chest to create a comfortable place to sit as well as storage for linens, sweaters, and other bulky items. Also try using room dividers, large plants, or bookcases to separate your dining area from your living area or home-office area. And instead of a full-sized couch and coffee table, try using a love seat or two recliners plus a set of smaller tables that can be moved around as needed or placed side by side to create a full-size coffee table to accommodate guests.

Tuesday: Think Vertical

🕐 15 minutes

The most underused space in any room is the two or three feet just below the ceiling, so in terms of shelving and storage, think vertical. If you have seven-foot ceilings, why buy a two- or three-foot-tall bookcase? Mount some shelves high up on the walls, over windows and doors, and above kitchen cabinets to make the most use of that precious space. When purchasing furniture and other items for your small living space, always think foldup, pullout, and multipurpose. For example, a tall coffee table can also function as a desk. A pullout couch can be used to sleep at night, but during the day it can double as a sofa.

Almost Perfect

Have everyone take off their outside shoes as soon as they set foot in your house. Keep a set of flip-flops or clogs by the door to slip on instead.

Wednesday: Add Some Color

🕐 15 minutes

An easy way to give your living room a makeover without sacrificing a whole day (or a whole bunch of money) is to make small, colorful additions to the space. A simple vase of brightly colored flowers is a far better decoration for your coffee table than a pile of magazines and newspapers. If your windows are bare, pick up some brightly colored curtains to add some interest to the room. Or add a funky lamp or eye-catching painting to the mix. As long as these colorful items don't clutter up valuable surfaces (such as tabletops and floor space), they make great additions to your living room.

Thursday: Banish Cleaning Tools and Products

🕐 10 minutes

If you think your vacuum cleaner adds to your living room's décor, think again. Vacuums, dusters, brooms, mops, buckets, air-freshening sprays, and any other cleaning tools or products have no place in your living room. Relocate these to a closet or laundry room where they won't be out in the open. If you have young children and find yourself constantly cleaning up spills and stains, keep a few dust cloths and maybe some upholstery cleaner tucked away in a drawer or cabinet in the living room. That way, you'll be able to grab these items quickly, but you won't have to pretend they're part of your decorating scheme.

Friday: Wrangle Your Rug

🕐 10 minutes

It may not seem like a big deal, but a living room rug that slides around on the floor can be a huge safety hazard—and can look really messy when it's scrunched up in one corner of the room. Children might slip and fall, and even you, the exceptionally coordinated adult of the house, can have an unbalanced day. Go to your local home goods or hardware store and pick up a rubber rug pad. These pads come in all shapes and sizes and can easily be cut with regular scissors if you need to fit an odd shape. Depending on the size of your rug, you'll probably be spending between $20 and $50 on the pad. If this sounds like a lot for something that will be hidden beneath a rug, consider the potential hospital bills if someone were to fall and suffer an injury.

Almost Perfect

Put down area rugs at all entry ways to cut down on dirt. If you're not tracking it in the house, you don't have to clean it up later on. In addition, have everyone hang up their coats as soon as they come in the house.

Saturday: Take Care of Your Wood-Burning Fireplace

🕐 **30 minutes**

Is your beautiful wood-burning fireplace dirty and somewhat unsafe? Today is the day to solve that problem. First, make sure you have high-quality fireplace implements; cheap substitutes can bend and burn and be a hazard when you're trying to adjust the position of larger, heavier logs. Get rid of any lingering ash or burnt logs and make sure you have a supply of fireplace necessities: long matches, firestarters, and logs nearby. Keep wood well stocked—no one wants to run outside in a snow storm to keep their living room cozy. Bring in a few logs at a time and place them in a bin beside your fireplace.

Almost Perfect

If you have a dirty fireplace, dip an old toothbrush in a water and bleach mix and do some scrubbing. This mixture will remove soot and breathe new life into your living room.

Sunday: Take Care of Your Gas Fireplace

🕐 10 minutes

While gas fireplaces require much less maintenance than their wood counterparts, you still want to maintain yours properly. Although gas fireplaces do not spark, move anything flammable (such as clothing, blankets, or pillows) away from the fireplace. If your fireplace has a glass door and the glass breaks, do not use the unit until the glass has been replaced. Follow any additional instructions in the owner's manual and make sure to have your fireplace inspected annually by a qualified professional service person (make an appointment today!), as gas leaks can be fatal.

Living Room Week 3

Monday: Get Ready for Guests

🕐 20 minutes

One of the benefits of getting your home in order is that your friends might actually be willing to visit you now! Put out the word that your abode is no longer a biohazard, and you might get some takers. If you hope that hosting might be in your future, invest in some extra sleeping materials for your living room. Keep it simple; your friends aren't moving in—and you don't want them to! Just pick up an air mattress and a cheap sheet/comforter set. Just make sure your guests deflate and put this stuff away in the morning. You don't need another catchall surface where clutter can accumulate.

Tuesday: Create Ambiance

🕒 20 minutes

The living room is all about comfort and relaxation, so here, more than anywhere else in your home, you want to have the right kind of lighting available to you. Do you like to read on the couch? Add a floor lamp or table lamp to one side. Do you like to watch movies with dim lighting? Install a dimmer switch to control the overhead lights. Is there one area of the room you'd like to highlight, such as a fireplace or piece of artwork? Consider installing recessed lighting or spotlights near these pieces. Are you a big fan of natural light? Replace those dusty blinds or heavy draperies with sheer curtains.

Wednesday: Stow Work Items

🕒 10 minutes

If you don't have a home office (or if you do but sometimes enjoy a change of scenery), you may be in the habit of bringing your laptop and paperwork into the living room every once in a while. This way, you can take care of business while still being with your family and enjoying another area of your home. The problem with this is that most people don't remove or hide the evidence when they're finished. If you're in the habit of leaving your laptop, briefcase, and other work materials in the living room, you're contributing to the clutter dilemma (as well as potentially stressing out family members who are trying to relax there). A solution is to designate a drawer, basket, or storage box for your work items: a power cord for your laptop, a pen, a pad of paper, a calculator, and so on. Take out the items when you sit down to work, and when you're finished, put them away.

Thursday: Display Your Photos

🕐 20 minutes

This is the *living* room, so what better place to display photos of you and your family doing just that? You might already store some photo albums in this room. If so, go pick out a few and hunt for your favorite pictures—from a vacation, a school play, or a summer barbecue. Once you've selected the best photos, choose a few frames that highlight the qualities of the images (the colors or settings) or that tie the images together. For instance, you can make any group of photos a collection just by displaying them in similar frames. If you don't have a lot of surface space, consider hanging your pictures on the wall. This will also draw the eye up, taking it away from any other clutter that might remain in the room.

Almost Perfect

If you're really low on space to display framed photos, or if you just happen to love technology, go out and get yourself a digital photo frame. This is a great way to display multiple photos without taking up lots of space in the room.

Friday: Go Natural

🕐 20 minutes

You've done so much great work to clean up and clear out your living room, and the last thing you want to do is add more "stuff." However, an addition you shouldn't shy away is some plant life. Choose just two or three plants to add color and life to the space without creating a cluttered look. You might select an indoor tree, such as a ficus or a tropical palm, or you might stick with smaller potted plants. If you want to place a plant up high on a shelf, consider getting a crawling plant, such as ivy or a spider plant. If you have a green thumb and know you'll keep on top of and enjoy plants, then give them a try. If not, there are some very lifelike fake plants out there. After all, a dead plant will *not* enhance the look of your living room.

Saturday: Throw It in the Trunk

🕐 10 minutes

Consider investing in an attractive storage trunk. While this may seem like an old-fashioned piece of furniture, it can actually hold a lot of items and lend an antique feel to the room. Go to a favorite antique store or thrift shop and ask if they have any trunks for sale. A trunk is an ideal place to store extra pillows and blankets, kids' toys, books, and magazines . . . almost anything! Just remember that this isn't an excuse to hoard junk. Only store what you need and either find a home for or get rid of the rest.

Sunday: Create a Game Center

🕐 20 minutes

If you have kids, chances are you also have dozens of games in your house, from board games like Monopoly and Candy Land to decks of cards and barrels of monkeys. A great way to keep all these games organized and in one place is to designate a spot for them. Purchase a small shelving unit for boxed games that stack neatly, and use a decorative bin or old-fashioned toy chest for those that are oddly shaped or have multiple parts. Teach your kids that their games will remain in good shape if they're taken care of and put away neatly. There's no reason why you shouldn't recruit your kids to help in your organization efforts.

Living Room Week 4

Monday: The Case Against the Case

🕐 **20 minutes**

If you have an extensive DVD collection but don't have space to store it, get rid of all the cases (sell them online or recycle) and store the individual discs in a CD book. You can have one big book and organize it alphabetically, keeping a typed list for easy use. Or you can keep several books by genre: one for dramas, one for action movies, one for comedies, and so on. If the books are attractive enough, you can just keep them on a bookshelf and pull them out when you need to find your next flick. This trick also works for CDs and video-game discs.

Tuesday: Be a Basket Case

🕐 **15 minutes**

Address the issue of kiddie clutter in the living room by giving each child his or her own basket. Over the course of the day, have your kids collect their action figures, storybooks, and dress-up clothes and place them in their individual baskets, leaving the room reasonably tidy. At the end of the day, have the kids bring their baskets to their bedrooms and put the items away. This will both foster their hunting and gathering skills and keep your living room from becoming a pigsty. To make this more fun, let each choose his favorite color or style: maybe pink baskets for girls and sports-themed baskets for boys.

Wednesday: Create an Illusion

🕐 10 minutes

If your living room is on the small side, try implementing a few optical illusions. For example, a dark color on the walls along with dark curtains and dark carpeting make a space feel smaller than it is. Try a lighter color that will reflect natural light and open up the space. We're not suggesting that you paint your whole living room (but you can if you'd like) but that you swap out dark fabrics for lighter ones. A striped rug, for instance, can serve to elongate a small room. Light-colored curtains can make a dark room brighter in just minutes. Stay away from busy patterns, though, as these can make a room feel full and boxed in.

Almost Perfect

Here's a trick that interior designers use: Paint the interior back wall of a bookcase (or the wall behind it if the bookcase has no back) a couple of shades deeper than the wall color in the room. For example, if the wall in your living room is a light sky blue, paint the inside of the bookcase a deeper turquoise. This will draw extra attention to your books and collectibles and make items pop against the contrasting backdrop.

Thursday: Guard Your Furniture

⏱ 5 minutes

You have pets. You have kids. You have a spouse who spills on the recliner or drools on the couch cushions after falling asleep after a long day at work. Clearly, it's time to protect your furniture from these domestic evils. Grab some Scotchgard Fabric and Upholstery Protector and go to town. All you have to do is spray and walk away. It will take your furniture about twenty-four hours to dry fully, so if you spray your furniture right before you head to bed everything should be dry when you get home from work tomorrow. If you have pets, you don't want them walking on the furniture while it dries, so find a way to keep them out of the room overnight.

Friday: Cool Down and Freshen Up

⏱ 5 minutes

If you're having company over on a hot summer day, you need a quick way to freshen up your living room before they arrive. Here's a quick tip that works every time. Turn on your floor or tabletop fan and set it to oscillate. Then take a fresh fabric softener sheet and place it on the backside of the fan. The force of the air will suck it in and make it stick to the fan. Then, as the fan circulates air and cools down the room, it will also infuse the air with the scent of clean laundry. Just one fabric softener sheet can freshen your living room for a whole day and make you forget that it's 95 degrees outside.

Saturday: Mirror, Mirror on the Wall

🕐 15 minutes

Mirrors are not only useful for the morning makeup routine, but they also brighten a room by reflecting light and make a room look bigger by projecting an image of the space in the room. Enhance your living room by hanging a mirror today. When deciding where to place it, however, consider what it will reflect. The reflection of another wall isn't going to do much for you, while a reflection of a window or pair of glass doors leading to a garden out back will make a huge difference in the way you see your living room.

Sunday: Living Room Bulletin

🕐 20 minutes

You may not believe it, but a bulletin board can be a great-looking and functional addition to your living room. Paint the frame a funky color if you want to spice it up, or if you're feeling especially motivated, cover it with fabric and make a memory board with your kids; you can find instructions anywhere online. Use your memory board to hang photos, cards (it's great around Christmastime!), or ticket stubs from concerts or plays you really enjoyed. Not only will this get clutter up off your furniture, it will also give you a chance to display mementos from your recent adventures. And don't just use regular old plastic pushpins. Instead, visit your jewelry box. Lost earrings are like lost socks in that they rarely resurface. So give those lovely orphaned earrings a new chance at life and use them as stylish alternatives to pushpins.

Living Room Week 5

Monday: Cover the Couch

🕐 20 minutes

Sick and tired of looking at that faded or stained couch upholstery but don't have the money for a replacement? The solution is a slipcover. You can find these at most home goods and discount stores, and if your couch is a standard size, you shouldn't have a problem finding one to fit. Choose a pattern or color that goes with your living room décor, and try to stay away from light colors that will show the dirt. Check the tag for washing instructions, and every few weeks throw the slipcover in the washing machine. In no time, your couch will look like new again!

Tuesday: Take Down Holiday Decorations

🕐 5 minutes

Okay, so it's not exactly the holiday season and you're sure you've removed all evidence of any other holiday. Check again. Are you sure there isn't a little white snowman peaking out from a cabinet sometime in July? A Fourth of July decoration still sparkling in February? The living room is probably one of the places in your home that gets the most attention during the holidays, and the danger with decorations is the tendency to leave them up for too long. If you find some stragglers, take them down now. And to avoid these tragic situations in the future, put away decorations within a week of the holiday's end. You won't miss them, and it'll allow you to look forward to the next holiday around the corner.

Wednesday: Clean the A/C Filter

🕒 10 minutes

Air in the living room feeling a little stale? It might be time to clean the filter in your air conditioner. This probably sounds like a time-consuming, annoying task, but really it's super simple. Just remove the filter (in newer models you can slide it right out using a tab) and run it under warm water in the sink. Make sure your drain guard is in place before you do it, though, as clumps of dust, lint, and hair could clog your pipes. When the filter is clean, pat it dry with a clean rag or a few paper towels and replace it. You won't be able to see a difference, but the improved air quality may improve any dust or pet hair allergies you or a family member might have.

Almost Perfect

If you and your family are eating in the living room, invest in trays. Keep your meals on the tray and avoid cleaning up spills and crumbs.

Thursday: Create a Music Space

🕒 20 minutes

If you're a member of a musical family, your living room may contain any number of instruments, books of music, tuning and amplification equipment, and other related items. These objects aren't clutter, but they can start to look and feel like it if they're kept in no particular order around the room. Today, designate one corner of your living room to music and use a large item, such as a piano, to anchor the space. Keep guitars on stands instead of in bulky cases, and place congas near a stool so people can sit down and start to play. Store any small items, such as tuners and guitar picks, in a decorative box or basket where you can grab them as needed. Play on!

Friday: Put It under Glass

🕐 15 minutes

If you have a coffee table with a glass top, use this as an opportunity to create a scrapbook-like display. Lift off the glass plate and arrange items on the coffee table. You might choose to include photos, ticket stubs, pressed flowers, wedding invitations . . . any flat items you'd like to see displayed on a regular basis. Once the items are placed where you want them, replace the glass to keep them there. When you tire of the collage you've made, simply remove the glass and start from scratch. This will not only keep paper clutter from accumulating in piles around your living room, but it will also give your family a customized piece of artwork to enjoy every day.

Saturday: Mix It Up

🕐 20 minutes

We've already established that shelves are a great storage solution for any room in the house, but the living room is where you can be most creative with how you organize them. Because you want living room storage to be both attractive and functional, try storing a variety of items neatly on the shelves. For example, place a stack of colorful paperbacks, spines facing out, next to a textured piece of pottery. A framed photo from one of your travels will complement a sculpture or vase you brought back with you from the trip. Move items around until the arrangement looks right, and dust shelves regularly to keep them looking their best. Also, be sure to retain some empty space on shelves to avoid a crowded appearance.

Sunday: Suck It Up

🕐 **15 minutes**

Vacuuming isn't the most thrilling chore in the world, but every once in a while you just have to do it. This is certainly the case when company is coming over; your guests don't need to tread on crumbs from movie popcorn, scraps from your last craft project, and dirt tracked in on the soles of shoes. The vacuum is the best choice for quick floor cleaning, regardless of whether you have carpeting, an area rug, or wood flooring in your living room. Most vacuums have different settings that can accommodate any situation. Vacuum the main traffic areas of the room, as well as the corners, and finish by sucking up any cobwebs near the ceiling.

Almost Perfect

If you have rugs, invest in a steamer and steam them clean once a month. This will freshen up your room, cut down on allergens, and make you more comfortable when you get down there to play with your pets or kids.

GET TO WORK: THE HOME OFFICE

You might be wondering, "Why do I have to organize my home office? No one sees it but me." Well, that's fine and dandy, as long as you don't mind swimming through a sea of paperwork, computer wires, and binder clips to get to work every day. Wouldn't it be nicer to sit down at a clean, orderly desk and start your work quickly, leaving more time for the important things and people in your life? Of course it would. So start cleaning.

Monday: Think about It

🕐 **20 minutes**

As you begin to put together a plan for this space, take some time to think about the types of work you'll be doing here. Will you be conducting all of your business from this location, or will you only be working from home one or two days a week? Will you mainly be communicating via the computer and the telephone, or will you also have visitors coming to meet with you? Do you need a lot of light to do your work, or perhaps a special feature like a bulletin board or lots of shelving? Give this room some serious thought and decide what will work best for you and your family.

Tuesday: Make a List (If You Can Find a Pen)

🕐 **20 minutes**

Develop a detailed list of furniture, equipment, and supplies that you need to have the home office of your dreams—or at least one you can stand to work in. Consider investing in furniture with plenty of drawers and filing cabinets with extra storage space. Issues such as lighting, ergonomics, and functionality all need to be addressed. As with any organizational task, planning is crucial, so put some thought into your needs and wants, and then address each issue individually.

Wednesday: Put on Your Designer Cap

🕐 **15 minutes**

Figure out how to lay out your home office so it will maximize your productivity and be a comfortable place to work. Because your desk is the central and most integral part of your home office, decide on its location first. Then determine what other furniture and equipment needs to be nearby and what can be placed elsewhere in the room. Try to position equipment close to electrical outlets and phone jacks, so you won't trip over a cord and put yourself out of commission.

Thursday: Let the Sunshine In!

🕐 20 minutes

If you have windows in your office, pull up the blinds! If the raw sunlight is too bright, pick up some sheer curtains, which will soften the light without blocking it out completely. Consider various options when choosing lamps, lighting fixtures, and light bulbs for your office. For example, fluorescent light bulbs may be cheaper and last longer, but they're much tougher on your eyes (and your mood) than traditional light bulbs. Plus, part of the luxury of working from home is that you can be productive without being forced to function in an industrial environment. Seize the freedom you have and make your office ideally suited to your own needs.

Friday: It's All about the Desk

🕐 20 minutes

The most important piece of furniture in any home office is the desk. You want your desk to be functional and comfortable, just the right height so that you don't have to hunch over it, with enough space to spread out your papers, and organized so you can find what you're looking for. Today's task is to either shop for or clean off your desk. As you shop around for the perfect desk, consider U-shaped or L-shaped designs that provide ample space for a computer, lamp, papers, and telephone but also give you space to do your work. If you're cleaning, make sure everything has a home and that it makes it back to its home at the end of each day.

Saturday: Get Creative with Storage

🕐 30 minutes

Utilize all of the available space in your home office to its greatest potential. For example, instead of having file bins on your desk, can you use hanging files and take advantage of nearby wall space? Try using a computer-monitor stand that has a shelf above and a drawer underneath to save valuable desk space. Office supplies, shipping supplies, and other items should be readily available. Consider purchasing drawer organizers to keep your office tools compartmentalized. For bulky items like industry magazines and articles, try dual-function furniture; perhaps you can store these inside an ottoman with a removable lid.

Sunday: Ready, Set, File!

$\bigcirc$ **45 minutes**

Files. You may have heard of these, but judging by the paper tornado sweeping through your office, you haven't quite gotten the hang of how filing works. Luckily, you've come to the right place. Here's what you do: Begin by creating a file (a file folder with a label tab) for each important paperwork category, such as Bank, Car, Health, Mortgage, and so on. Then when you find a paper with no home, decide where it belongs and put it in that file. It's that easy! You'll want to create files for most of your office papers, though your most time-sensitive and important papers can be kept directly on your desk. The trick, however, is to be disciplined enough to process those important papers promptly so that they don't accumulate and take over.

Home Office Week 2

Monday: Say Ta-Ta to Trinkets

$\bigcirc$ **15 minutes**

One group of items that always seem to end up in the office but don't really belong there are the trinkets and other little keepsakes that don't have anything to do with your business. You want your office to have a personal touch, but that miniature Christmas tree you forgot to put away after the holidays and vase of dead flowers are only compounding your clutter problem. Keep sentimental items on your desk to a minimum—a family photo and a #1 Dad mug, for example—and move the rest to another surface in the room. Not only will this help you focus on your work, but you'll have fewer things to dust as well!

Tuesday: Cut 'Em Out

🕐 20 minutes

Are you a magazine and newspaper hoarder? Do you have yourself convinced that one of these days you really will make time to read them all? That's a lovely dream, but it ain't gonna happen. Instead of keeping every full issue, flip through and cut out the articles that interest you and put them in a labeled folder for future—and I mean near future—reading. If you end up with lots of articles, get a folder with multiple pockets and give them all labels, such as Arts, Economy, Local, Recipes, and so on. That way you'll know where to go first when the mood strikes.

Almost Perfect

Instead of having extension cords and outlet extenders all over the place, simplify with a surge protector. This will keep all your plugs nice and neat, and protect against electrical surges. Check the back to make sure it's UL listed and is a transient voltage surge protector.

Wednesday: Play a Game of Toss and Keep

🕐 25 minutes

If you've been saving all your electric utility statements and cancelled checks since 1985, it's time to adopt a new system. It's extremely unlikely that you'll ever need proof of payment of utility bills and the like, so you really only need to keep the most recent few months' worth on hand. Likewise, ATM and bank statements can be tossed as soon as you've noted the amounts in your records and reconciled the information with your accounts. Even better, take some time today and enroll in online bill pay. A lot of companies and banks will e-mail you your statements that you can then save on your computer.

Thursday: Liberate Yourself with a Paper Shredder

🕐 20 minutes

If you've never used a paper shredder before, you don't know what you're missing. This fabulous machine takes all those extraneous stacks of papers all over your office and transforms them into long paper shreds. This may not sound that thrilling in itself, but here's the good part: With a paper shredder, you can finally get rid of all those old documents you've been afraid to toss because they contain personal information. Once you've shredded them beyond recognition, throw them in the recycling bin and send them on their way.

Friday: Clean That Screen

🕐 5 minutes

Computer screen looking a little dull? Time to wipe it down. But before you reach for the paper towels, note that computer screens are very delicate and can be damaged if the wrong cleaner or too much pressure is applied. First establish whether you have cathode-ray tube (CRT) monitor, which is a glass screen, or a liquid-crystal display (LCD) screen. In both cases you want to use a very soft antistatic cloth, and you want to spray the cleaning solution onto the cloth, never directly on the screen. For a CRT monitor, spray a modest amount of glass cleaner, such as Windex, on the cloth and then gently wipe the screen. For an LCD screen, spray a solution of one part rubbing alcohol or cider vinegar and one part water onto the cloth and then gently wipe the screen. Wipe it once more with a soft, dry cloth, and you're done!

Saturday: Break It Up

🕒 **25 minutes**

One way to make sure things stay in their proper places in your home office is to establish zones. For example, you might have a work zone that includes a clear work surface, your computer, and regularly used office supplies; a reference zone where books, magazines, and other such materials are kept; and a supply zone where you store your paperclips, envelopes, staples, and so on. If any of these items tries to sneak out of its zone and into another, chase it back where it belongs. When everything is in its proper place, you'll always know where to find what you need.

Sunday: Keep Some, Store the Rest

🕒 **20 minutes**

We know you're tempted to keep all the documents that have ever graced your home office where you can readily access them, but when was the last time you needed to? Keep only the documents you truly need in your office space and only the current year's files. Box up any receipts, statements, or miscellaneous paperwork older than that and put it in long-term storage, perhaps the basement, attic, or a hall closet. Put each year's documents in a separate box and mark the year clearly on the outside. Once you've reached the end of the time you need to save a certain year (maybe 5–7 years out), just toss or recycle the whole box! Exceptions to the rule are medical files, veterinarian records, and car repair records. It's a good idea to keep those relatively handy, even if they're a few years old.

Home Office Week 3

Monday: Purge Digital Clutter

🕐 15 minutes

The tangible items in your home office aren't the only ones that need organizing. Your computer's hard drive might also be a mess of unlabeled files, documents with no home, and resources that aren't orderly or accessible. If you suspect this might be the case, sit down at your computer and survey the situation. If your desktop is littered with random documents, take a few minutes and create some folders for them. Do you have a bunch of large photo or video files that you no longer need? Toss 'em! They're taking up valuable space on your hard drive and also making it difficult for you to focus on the task at hand.

Tuesday: Clean Your Keyboard

🕐 10 minutes

Ever taken a close look at your computer keyboard? Gross, right? That thing is essentially a trap for dust and dirt. Why does this matter? Well, not only can crumbs and other obstructions clog up your keys' depression space, but every time you touch your keyboard you could be picking up bacteria. Don't freak out; there's an easy fix here. To clean your keyboard, hold it upside down and run a dry watercolor paintbrush between the keys to loosen dirt and dust. Certain models also have removable keys that pop right off with the use of your fingernail so you can clean beneath them.

Wednesday: Recycle Where You Work

🕐 5 minutes

There's no reason why you can't do your job and look after Mother Earth at the same time. But if you have to walk to some other part of the house to reach the recycling bin, you might be tempted to just toss recyclable paper in the garbage—or keep in a pile to get to later. We're not calling you lazy (at least not to your face), but it is human nature to take the path of least resistance. Make it easy to do the right thing and keep a paper recycling bin right in your office, either next to your garbage can or near the copy or fax machine where you think it will be most useful. Empty it when you take out your other recyclables once a week so it doesn't overflow.

Thursday: Make Do with a Minifridge

🕐 20 minutes

Think back to your college days. Do you remember the minifridge in your freshman dorm room? Back then, you probably kept it stocked with cheap beer and string cheese; those days are far behind you, right? Right. But even though you're not an undergrad anymore, a minifridge might still have a place in your life. Do you often wish you had a cold drink or a snack within easy reach while you're plugging away in your home office? A minifridge can make this dream come true—and reduce clutter. If you have a place to keep beverages and snacks, they're less likely to end up littering your desk. Just make sure you use your minifridge for brain food!

Friday: Snail Mail the Smart Way

🕐 15 minutes

If your business requires you to send out lots of mail, set up a mailing station. Your station should include plenty of stamps so you don't have to run to the post office in the middle of the day; a letter opener; envelopes of various sizes; an envelope moistener with adhesive, to save your tongue some labor; and any other mailing items you use regularly. If you send out more than ten pieces of mail a day, you might consider investing in a postage meter. This takes away the need for stamps by allowing you to print out postage as you need it, drawing from an account that you replenish on a regular basis.

Saturday: Recycle Old Printer Cartridges

🕐 15 minutes

You've probably heard that you shouldn't throw printer cartridges for inkjet printers in the trash. What the heck are you supposed to do with them then? Recycling is the answer. Most manufacturers have programs that allow you to mail the cartridges back to them singly or several at a time for proper recycling. Some even come with packaging with prepaid postage for this very purpose. Easy, right? So get those old, empty cartridges out of your home office, and do your part to keep them out of the landfill as well.

Sunday: Ditch the CDs

🕒 20 minutes

It wasn't that long ago that everyone used blank CDs for everything, from transferring files to burning music and movies. But these days you can accomplish these tasks digitally or with a flash drive or portable hard drive. To reduce clutter in your home office, get with the times! Upload any important materials from those burned CDs and then throw them away. They're only getting dusty sitting on your desk, and it's time you gave them the heave ho. If you feel the need to keep certain CDs for your records, put them into storage files and stow them away.

Almost Perfect

Make a list of the items that you struggle with and, as a family, come up with solutions. If there are too many books lying around, get a library card. If you have too many CDs, load your music onto an iPod.

Home Office Week 4

Monday: Post It on a Bulletin Board

🕒 10 minutes

In the home office, a bulletin board is a great place to post reminders, a calendar, and important phone numbers and email addresses. Hang your bulletin board on the wall next to your desk where you can easily access it and see it from you chair. If it's not in a good location, you won't use it, and it'll become just one more thing cluttering up your office.

Tuesday: Write It on a White Board

🕐 10 minutes

These days it's all about the white board. Similar to a bulletin board, this can hang near your desk and function as a place to jot down ideas and reminders, or to work out complicated problems in writing. Your notes can stay up there as long as you like, and then all it takes is a swipe of an eraser to bring you back to a clean slate. You can find white boards and white board markers at any office supply store.

> ### *Almost Perfect*
>
> New blinds or drapes can have a striking visual effect on the atmosphere of your office. If you like what you have or don't want to spend the money on new window treatments right now, simply opt for a cleaning. This will brighten your curtains and leave the room smelling clean and fresh.

Wednesday: Dust

🕐 15 minutes

Yes, your home office gets just as dusty as the rest of the rooms in your home. Maybe more so because you're less likely to want to spend time in there once your workday is done. Take a few minutes and get the dusting out of the way. Your office is pretty likely to have a variety of smallish things that need dusting: your office phone, computer stand, file holders, and so on. An easy way to dust these oddly shaped items is to spray some Pledge or Endust on an old fabric glove or mitten and just run your hand over anything and everything that you see (but not the computer monitor. See "Clean That Screen"). When you're done dusting, take the glove off and toss it in the wash.

Thursday: The Handy-Dandy Desk Calendar

⏱ 10 minutes

You may have your Blackberry or cell phone alarm set to go off when you have an upcoming appointment or meeting, but when it comes to office organization, nothing beats a backup. What if your cell phone battery dies and you can't find your charger? Desk calendar to the rescue! It's flat, so it won't take up any space in your office; you can perform tasks right on top of it, as if it's part of your desk. And most desk calendars are nice and big, with lots of room to write down notes and specifics for appointments.

Friday: Give Your Desk the Reach Test

⏱ 10 minutes

You've done a lot of work to clean and organize your home office, so things should be in pretty good shape. To make sure, administer the reach test. Sit at your new and improved desk and start doing some work. Is everything you need within easy reach? For example, you should not have to get up and leave your desk to staple something. Adjust your office design as necessary, moving the items or equipment you use most often to a location closer to you. Take note of what you don't use, too. Items you don't use often should be stored in a drawer or on a shelf farther away.

Saturday: Get Uplifted

🕐 5 minutes

A great way to save your neck and give yourself a little more room/storage on your desk is to buy yourself a computer-monitor stand. These often come with a shelf above and a drawer underneath where you can store office supplies or paperwork. They also ensure that your computer monitor will be at eye level and thus inflict less stress on your neck, shoulders, and arms. After all, you're working from home so you may as well be as comfortable as possible, right? Also, if you happen to spill something on your newly cleaned desk—coffee, juice, water— the stand will put your monitor, and all the important info therein, out of harm's way.

Sunday: Rest Your Eyes

🕐 10 minutes

Sitting at a computer all day can be tiring, regardless of the lack of physical activity involved. A sedentary job can be tough on all parts of your body, from your neck to your lower back, but a computer screen is especially hard on the eyes. To keep your eyes from aching, give them a place to rest every so often. This might be a soothing watercolor painting that you hang on the wall across from your desk or a beautiful potted plant that sits on the windowsill. When you feel your eyes begin to strain, move them to your soothing spot. After a few minutes you'll feel refreshed and ready to continue. Adding some artwork to your home office will also make the room look more professional. We're not talking about one of those "Teamwork!" posters, either. Choose photography, watercolors, or another type of art that you love to look at. You're the boss, after all.

YOUR BEDROOM IS YOUR SANCTUARY

The bedroom. Sounds simple; just a room with a bed in it, right? Unfortunately, this room often becomes a catchall—for clothes, shoes, reading materials, purses, briefcases, dog toys, mugs from last night's tea . . . you name it. Because you spend most of your time in this room unconscious, it's easy to let it get out of control. But this space is just as important as any other room in your home. And let's be honest: You're doing a lot more than sleeping in here and nothing kills a romantic buzz more than an unmade bed and clothes all over the floor.

Bedroom Week 1

Monday: Start with Surfaces

🕐 20 minutes

Today let's pay attention to flat surfaces. Dressers, nightstands, bookcases . . . these surfaces just have a way of becoming cluttered to the nines. You'll probably find everything from hairbrushes and nail clippers to reading glasses and romance novels. Without thinking too long about each individual item, start to put things away: clothes in drawers, nail clippers in the bathroom, romance novels in the bookcase. Once these surfaces are clear, your bedroom will appear bigger, cleaner, and more comfortable—and all in just twenty minutes.

Tuesday: Round Up Those Shoes

🕐 20 minutes

Shoes are great, and everyone needs more than a few pairs. But you have to draw the line somewhere. If they're everywhere in your bedroom—scattered under the bed, in piles in the closet, and dotting the floor like land mines—it's time to take action. Round up those wild, roaming shoes and you'll see an instant improvement in the appearance of your bedroom. Once you've done so, evaluate each pair and ask yourself some questions: When was the last time you wore these? Are they damaged, ill fitting, or smelling to high heaven? Old pairs you don't wear anymore have no place in your bedroom—or even your home. If they're still in decent shape, donate them. If they're beyond resurrection, throw them away.

Wednesday: Rack 'Em!

🕐 10 minutes

If you've cut back on the amount of shoes in your bedroom (see, "Round Up Those Shoes"), it's time to take another step forward. If you're still suffering from shoe madness, you need a shoe rack to help you keep your sandals, sneakers, and stilettos under control. There are several styles. You might choose an over-the-door shoe holder that hangs on the inside of your closet or a free-standing shoe rack that will fit somewhere out of the way, such as on the floor of your closet. Just arrange the shoes in the pockets of the holder or slide them over the pegs in the rack. This way, you'll always know where they are at all times, and you won't risk breaking your neck on your favorite pair when you get up to go to the bathroom in the middle of the night.

Thursday: The Cure for Clothing Chaos

🕐 20 minutes

Wrinkled skirts or dress pants, jogging shorts and sports bras, dirty socks and pajamas—they're all balled up on the floor, or hanging over your bed's footboard, or piled in a heap on your reading chair. This simply will not do. What you need is a hamper. Put it in a place where you'll see it (and remember about its existence) at the beginning and end of each day. Dirty clothes should go directly in the hamper after wearing. And for those items you can wear more than once before washing, such as sweatshirts or outerwear, you'll need a system for those, too. Our suggestion is a double hamper, with one side for dirty clothes and the other for those that are still in circulation.

Friday: Stop Getting Fleeced

🕐 10 minutes

Unless you live in Antarctica, you don't need all those throw pillows, fleece blankets, afghans, quilts, and Snuggies out at all times. If you use all of these on a constant basis, it might be time to turn up the heat! In a home that is kept above freezing you only need a couple of pillows and a blanket or two on your bed, and that's it. All those other comfy items strewn around your bedroom are only making the space look sloppy. Fold them and put them away in a closet or chest until you need them, and when you're done using them, for heaven's sake, fold and stow them again. This quick cleanup move will make a huge difference in how your bedroom looks.

Almost Perfect

If you own six sets of sheets for your one bed, you may have gone a little overboard. All those extra sheets and pillowcases take up valuable storage space that you could be using for other things. Two sets of high-quality sheets are plenty, and you can simply rotate them when you do laundry. If you live in a cold climate, you might also keep an extra set of flannel sheets on hand for those biting winter nights.

Saturday: Throw It in the Basket

🕐 20 minutes

Here's a really quick and easy way to tackle clutter: Buy yourself a big, attractive basket to keep somewhere in your bedroom—next to your nightstand or your dresser, perhaps. Throughout the week, instead of leaving a trail of clutter all over your room, just drop items you don't have time to put away into the basket. Then, once a week, take a few minutes to sort through the basket's contents, putting each item back in its proper place. This will keep the clutter confined to one space (and hidden inside a good-looking container) until you have time to deal with it.

Sunday: Set Up a Station

🕐 25 minutes

Your bedroom is mainly meant for sleeping, but if you're like most people, you probably end up bringing other tasks into bed with you, such as reading, writing to-do lists, or browsing through catalogs. Instead of keeping pens and reading materials scattered throughout the room, pick a spot—the drawer of your nightstand would be a good choice—where you can keep these items centralized. Gather a few pens and pencils and a pair of scissors, a couple of books and magazines you intend to read soon, and a pad of notepaper. This way, when you're ready to do a little reading or writing before bed, you'll know exactly where to find your materials—and where to put them when you're done.

Bedroom Week 2

Monday: Freshen Up, Effortlessly

🕐 5 minutes

Linen and upholstery fresheners, such as Febreze, offer an easy way to give your bedroom a clean feel without lifting a finger. Simply spray your comforter and pillows and any upholstered furniture in the room, and take a whiff. Smells like you just did laundry, right? There are also special closet sprays that keep hanging clothes fresh and aromatherapy linen sprays for use on your pillows before you get into bed at night. Lavender is a calming scent that is commonly used to promote deep, restful sleep. Just spray your pillow, give it a few moments to work its way into the fibers of the fabric, and then lay down your weary head. By morning you'll feel completely refreshed—and so will your bedroom!

Tuesday: Please Rise

🕐 15 minutes

If you've already done some purging in your bedroom but you find you still don't have enough space for your belongings, it's time to take your storage strategy to the next level, literally. Go to your local home goods store and pick up a set of bed risers. These are wooden or plastic blocks that go beneath the four legs of your bed, raising it higher and creating more space underneath it. These extra inches allow you to store (and hide) plastic storage containers, shoe boxes, suitcases—items you don't need at the ready at all times but that aren't quite suitable for basement or attic storage.

Wednesday: Do a Dust Ruffle

🕐 15 minutes

If you're using the space beneath your bed for storage, you may want to invest in a dust ruffle (also called a bed skirt). It's essentially a little curtain that keeps the space under your bed hidden from view, allowing you to fully utilize your newfound storage space. If you get one that matches your bedding, it will add an extra aesthetic touch without much extra effort. All you do is spread out the dust ruffle between your mattress and box spring. Just make sure you get one long enough to hide your under-the-bed storage.

Thursday: Tame a Wandering Wardrobe

🕐 15 minutes

Got a wardrobe that doesn't respect the boundaries of your closet? Well, you might just have too many garments packed in there. To make your clothes a little more comfortable, put winter items into storage for the summer and vice versa. Keep them in a container under your bed or in a suitcase you're not using. Clear plastic containers are especially great since all it takes is a quick peek under the bed to know what's there. Then when that change of seasons comes, simply swap them out.

Almost Perfect

Love boots? If so, you might be the perfect candidate for boot shapers. These are inserts that go inside your boots and keep their shape when you're not wearing them. Boot shapers come in both inflatable and spring-loaded designs to fit any boot height, and some even have integrated hooks so you can hang them from a closet rod.

Friday: Hang 'Em High

🕐 15 minutes

Forget wire. The world of hangers is incredibly sophisticated these days with all manner of materials and styles available.

There are wide plastic hangers with rounded shoulders for jackets and sweaters that need to keep their shape. There are hangers with tiers that can hold several pairs of pants at once. You can get a special hanger for belts, another for handbags, and another for ties. Hangers made from cedar wood naturally repel pests like moths that are attracted to your outfits. Now all you need is a hanger that compliments you on your fashion choices and you'll be all set. Pick up some new hangers and spend a few minutes putting them into use.

Saturday: Hide the Jewels!

🕐 15 minutes

Don't worry—there isn't a jewel thief on the loose. This tip refers to a different kind of crime: the oodles of necklaces, bracelets, earrings, and other jewelry currently cluttering the top of your dresser or vanity. This glittery mess probably won't land you in jail, but it does contribute to your bedroom's chaotic appearance. The solution is not rocket science; it's a jewelry box. Choose one that is attractive and fits your décor, but more importantly, be sure it fits your needs. For example, if you have a lot of necklaces, select a box with enough drawer space or hooks for them. If you're an earring enthusiast, you need a jewelry box with spots for various styles—from studs and hoops to drop earrings.

Almost Perfect

If you don't have room for a jewelry box, install a few small hooks above your vanity. Hang your necklaces here to keep them from sitting in tangled piles somewhere else.

Sunday: It's in the Bag!

10 minutes

Purses and bags taking over your bedroom and closet? Here's an easy storage trick: Put the bags inside one another, like Russian nesting dolls, beginning with the smallest and moving up to the biggest. For example, take a clutch and place it inside a purse; take the purse and place it inside a shoulder bag; and so on. By the time you're done, you'll have just one bag to store instead of several. You can keep it on a shelf in your closet or under your bed and out of sight. This way, you'll always know exactly where to find the bag you're looking for.

Bedroom Week 3

Monday: Do the Hanger Test

10 minutes

If you're a clotheshorse, you may have trouble recognizing which clothes you wear and which you don't. To find out, try this trick: Turn all of the hangers in your closet around so that the point of the hook faces you instead of the back of the closet. When you wear and launder something, hang the hanger up as usual with the hook facing away from you. At the end of the season, survey the hanger situation. What do you see? If there are a lot of hangers tips still facing you, think seriously about donating anything you haven't worn. You may be surprised by how much unworn clothing you're storing in that closet!

Tuesday: Lint-Roll Your Lampshades

⏱ 10 minutes

You may have noticed that lampshades get dustier more quickly than almost any other surface in the house. They're like dust magnets, and traditional dusting tools don't seem to do a thing. Don't even bother with dusters; go find your lint roller or lint brush. If you don't have one, go to any home goods store and pick one up. There are two common styles: one with disposable adhesive sheets and another that you clean by hand and use over and over. Either is fine. Once you've got it, roll your lampshade the way you would a garment to remove dust, lint, and pet hair. It works like a charm!

Wednesday: Give Your Dresser a Sense of Purpose

⏱ 20 minutes

Hopefully the flat surfaces in your bedroom are clear (if not, check out "Start with Surfaces"), and with any luck that includes the top of your dresser. But now that it's a blank slate, you need to decide what the best use is for this surface. Will it be a vanity of sorts, with a mirror, jewelry box, and makeup kit? Or will you use this space to store items like lotion and perfume? If your dresser is next to your bed, it might function like a nightstand—a spot for reading materials, reading glasses, and other related items. Whatever purpose you choose for the top of your dresser, always keep it neat and dusted. Once you start using it as a dumping ground, you'll find yourself back in Clutterville.

Thursday: Create a Cozy Nook

⏱ **20 minutes**

You probably had the best of intentions when you put that comfy chair in the corner of your bedroom, but what was meant to be a relaxing space has turned into a mound of madness. Don't fret; some good old-fashioned organization can fix this. Begin by removing anything that doesn't have to do with relaxing—put away clothes, shoes, bags, and so on. Then place a side table with drawers and shelves next to your chair to help keep piles of books or balls of yarn or whatever it is that you're into off the floor. Make sure you have less things on your shelves or in your drawers than could actually fit there. This isn't so you'll have room to fill up your space later on either; it's to create a spacious, airy, relaxing look that will help your room feel the same.

Almost Perfect

Looking for more ways to bring a sense of calm and peace to your bedroom? Try scented candles or incense. Certain scents, such as lavender and jasmine, have long been used to promote sleep, and the dim candlelight will likely make your eyelids feel heavy. Incense, which releases fragrant smoke when burned, is another option to calm the senses and prepare for a good night's sleep.

Friday: Make Your Bed

⏱ **5 minutes**

Remember when Mom used to force you to make your bed each morning? She wasn't trying to torture you; she was onto something. Your bed is the central object in this room, so its condition will automatically rub off on everything around it. A nicely made bed promotes a feeling of calm in your bedroom, which will in turn rub off on you! Of course, some days are busier than others, and you won't always have time to do a perfect job of it. On those occasions, just pull up the covers and straighten the pillows.

Saturday: Take It Drawer by Drawer

🕐 30 minutes

Even if the outside of your dresser is clean and organized (See "Start with Surfaces"), it doesn't mean that the inside is off the hook. Depending on how many drawers you have, this may seem like huge task. But it doesn't have to be. To begin, decide which drawers will hold which items. Most people choose to keep items like bras, underwear, and socks in a top drawer, T-shirts in a drawer below that, and pants on the bottom. If you have more drawers to work with, you might use one for workout gear and another for pajamas and lounging clothes. Garments don't have to be perfectly folded at all times—although that will cut back on wrinkles . . . and subsequent ironing—but you should at least make sure that nothing is spilling out the sides.

Sunday: Phone a Friend

🕐 30 minutes

If you're having trouble parting with old or unworn clothes, it's time to call for reinforcements. Pick up the phone and invite over a friend who will give it to you straight. Her presence alone will help you see that those pumps with the worn-down heels are really past their prime and that blouse from college doesn't quite fit anymore. In no time you'll be tossing items into the donate or trash pile. When you have a friend there to help you make decisions, you'll see items through their eyes in addition to your own. And a little perspective goes a long way toward clearing your bedroom of clutter.

Almost Perfect

Twice a year or once a season, go through your clothes and weed out what you're not wearing. Have Big Brother, Big Sister, or the Salvation Army come pick up what you don't need.

Bedroom Week 4

Monday: Master Your Domain

⏱ **10 minutes**

You are the master of your domain, as evidenced by the fact that you live in the master bedroom. Most master bedrooms include an adjoining bathroom, which is a wonderful feature indeed. However, it can also come with a side effect: laziness. Do you find that bathroom items are creeping into the bedroom and vice versa? Doesn't look good, does it? Strewn towels and toiletries will make your bedroom look sloppy, and dirty clothes and kicked-off shoes will do the same to your bathroom. It's time to draw the line. Keep items where they belong, and your rooms will look neater. Plus you'll always know where to find things.

Tuesday: Hide a Secret Scent

10 minutes

A nice, inviting scent can go a long way toward making a room feel fresh and clean. If you don't have time to do a deep clean on your bedroom, just slip a sachet inside each of your pillowcases. You can buy premade sachets at most home goods and department stores, or you can make your own. To do this, first go to a crafts store and buy some potpourri. Choose a scent that you find comforting, such as apple cinnamon or honey vanilla. Then take a pair of old nylons and cut them at the ankle. Fill the nylons three-quarters of the way with potpourri and then tie them off. Once they're in the pillowcases you won't be able to see them, but you will smell the difference!

Wednesday: Dust the Ceiling Fan

5 minutes

The bedroom is one place where it's super simple to dust a ceiling fan. Why? Because all you have to do is stand on the bed to reach it. Before you begin, make sure the fan and light fixture are switched off. Lay a towel down on your bed to catch any falling dust. Then grab a rag or feather duster and climb on up there. Once the fan is within reach, give each fan blade a good wipe-down, and also run the duster over any light fixtures. This is also a good opportunity to check fixtures for dead bugs and dead bulbs. The whole task shouldn't take more than five quick minutes.

Thursday: Clean Your Secret Junk Drawer

⏱ 20 minutes

That's right. We're onto you. While junk drawers are most commonly found in the kitchen and home office, they can also pop up in your dresser or nightstand. And like your other junk drawers, you have to clean this one out too. To begin, empty out the drawer and see what you've got. Toss any trash and unwanted items, and remove anything that doesn't belong here. Next, get yourself an organizer tray. You might choose one just like what you use for silverware in the kitchen or something similar to what you have in your home office. Whatever tray you choose, make sure it has lots of compartments for all the various items you'll be storing in this drawer. The idea is to be able to open it and quickly find what you need, not rummage through a mess of, well, junk.

Almost Perfect

A quick and easy way to make your bedroom look clean is to dust your bed frame. Your headboard and footboard accumulate dust over time, so it's best to run a feather duster or damp cloth over them every few weeks. Also quickly dust between the bed and the wall in case any cobwebs have appeared there. You may find you breathe easier at night once the dust is gone.

Friday: Take a Close Look at Your Bed

⏱ 5 minutes

When you look at your bed, what do you see? Blankets? A huge comforter? Pillows, pillows, and more pillows? Yes, pillows are pretty, but let's get real. You're not the princess and the pea, and you don't live in a hotel. Keep your bedding simple: you only needs sheets, a blanket, a comforter, and the pillows you actually use. Extra pillows look pretty on the bed, but it won't take long before you're sick of putting them back there each morning. Take your extra pillows and either store them for guests or donate them to a worthy, comfort-loving cause.

Saturday: Don't Forget the Door

🕐 20 minutes

The inside of a closet door is one of the best places to create extra storage in your bedroom, and these days there are all sorts of tools that will help you do it. If you're a frequent Container Store shopper, you've probably seen products made by elfa, a Swedish company that manufactures simple and well-designed storage systems. One such item that you might look into is the elfa Pantry Door & Wall Rack. This is essentially a rod that attaches to the inside of your closet door and holds baskets of various sizes. While this is designed for pantries, it's also great for holding bedroom items, from lotions and perfumes to books and CDs. Most Container Stores will even send someone to your house to install it for you—for a fee, of course.

Sunday: Add Some Fresh Flowers

🕐 15 minutes

Potted plants are nice and all, but they do require maintenance. An easier option for giving your bedroom a punch of color and a natural touch are fresh-cut flowers. The next time you're at the grocery store, visit the florist and pick up a bouquet of daisies, lilies, roses, or whatever your heart desires. If you know in your heart that these flowers will die and linger in your bedroom, just make it easy for yourself from the get-go and buy fake flowers instead. They'll last year round and you never have to replace them . . . just be sure to dust them off once in a while. No matter what type of flowers you choose, place them on top of your dresser or nightstand, or near a window where their colors will be most brilliant in the sunlight.

Bedroom Week 5

Monday: Control Remote Chaos

🕐 10 minutes

If you watch TV in your bedroom, you may have a bit of a remote control proliferation on your hands. You don't have to ditch any of your electronics (though now might be a good time to simplify if you have the desire), but you would benefit from a system for keeping all these remotes under control. The solution is simple. Devote a drawer in your nightstand to this purpose, or use a decorative basket near your bed to hold the remotes. Either way, if they're kept together they won't become part of the clutter problem, and you'll always know where to find them. You can also condense down to a universal remote if you're so inclined.

Tuesday: Keep It Travel Sized

🕐 10 minutes

Are lotions and perfumes taking over your bedroom? If you're someone who uses a different type of moisturizer for every part of your body or wears various different kinds of perfume depending on your mood, these items may hang out all over the place. One solution to this problem is to just move these items to the bathroom where they can be kept organized in a cabinet. But if you really want them in your boudoir, keep little travel-size containers of them in the bedroom and the larger bottles behind closed doors. When they run low, you can just fill them up from the master supply.

Wednesday: Sleep in Peace

🕐 15 minutes

If you're having trouble falling asleep at night, there could be multiple causes. The plummeting stock market or global warming could be part of the problem, but this is the wrong book for that. Instead, our suggestion for sound sleep concerns the décor. If you use your bedroom for multiple purposes, from reading to ironing, you might find it hard to relax at bedtime with all those other tools and items in your periphery. Get them out of sight and out of mind by using a screen or room divider, or by hanging a curtain around your bed. That way, when you enter the sleeping area, you can put all other thoughts behind you—literally.

Almost Perfect

Only use your bedroom for sleeping and sex. Get rid of anything that doesn't help with either.

Thursday: Save Linen Packaging

🕐 10 minutes

You know those plastic zipper cases that sheets, pillows, and comforters come in? While your impulse may be to throw these away after you remove the bedding, resist this urge. Instead, keep these cases for a number of uses. For one, you can use these to store the bedding when hot summer weather comes or to store other winter garments such as thick socks, gloves, hats, and scarves. Because the packages are made of clear plastic, you'll easily be able to see what's inside at a glance.

Friday: Have a Shoe Photo Shoot

🕐 20 minutes

Some people like to save the shoeboxes their shoes came in for easy, stackable storage. If you're down with this, and you have the space to spare in your closet, go for it! But take it a step further. Take a photo of each pair and affix it to the outside of the shoebox. This way, you can easily see which pairs are in which boxes for easy grabbing. This will also make deciding which pair to wear a snap. If you have on a yellow dress, you can just look up, see the image of the yellow, strappy sandals, and pull down the right box.

Saturday: Try Over-the-Bed Shelving

🕐 30 minutes

You've seen over-the-toilet shelving, right? Well, here's a similar idea, with fewer germs. Over-the-bed shelving is a great space saver, and it puts items such as books, reading glasses, and alarm clocks right at your fingertips. Most over-the-bed shelving units come boxed, with simple instructions for do-it-yourself assembly. This makes it easy to assemble the unit around your bed, rather than having to wrestle with an already-assembled hunk of furniture. Once the unit is in place, be selective about what you store there. If you're not careful, this can become a catchall for clutter and junk!

Sunday: Doll Up Your Dresser

🕐 20 minutes

Tired of looking at that same old dresser year after year but don't have the money or a good enough reason to replace it? Our suggestion is to go to your local hardware or home goods store and pick out new drawer pulls. Far less work and less expensive than putting on a new coat of paint or replacing the dresser entirely, new drawer pulls will completely change the look of your dresser in no time. Just make sure you get pulls that will fit the holes that are already there. Then simply unscrew the old ones and screw in the new ones. Voila! A dresser makeover in minutes.

LOOK AT THIS PIGSTY! THE KIDS' ROOMS

You've seen a mess or two in your day, but chances are you've never encountered something quite like this. Yes, your lovely little darlings created this disaster, and no, you can't put them on the street with Free signs around their necks. But you *can* do that with some of their old toys, clothes, and other clutter. Follow this chapter's simple steps to get your kids' rooms back in order.

Monday: Lay Down the Law

🕐 20 minutes

When you look at your kids's rooms, you're probably tempted to just do the cleaning yourself. But whatever you do, resist this urge! Your kids will never learn the value and importance of cleaning up after themselves if you do it for them. Instead, take some time today to tell them that from here on out they will be expected to put away their toys and clothes as soon as they're done using or wearing them. Point out which areas of the room you want them to give special attention: the beds, the closets, and the floor space, perhaps. Get them on board by offering an incentive such as a a special treat to reward them for a job well done.

Tuesday: Get Down

🕐 20 minutes

Kids are lower to the ground than you are, so it helps to get down to their level and see what things look like from there. What's in and out of reach? When organizing the kids' rooms, start from the bottom and work your way to the top. Favorite toys and games should be kept on lower shelves where your kids can easily reach them. Items that are used less often, and those that are breakable or valuable, should be kept up high where only you can access them. As kids get older (and taller), you can rearrange this setup as necessary.

Wednesday: Go Topless

⏱ 15 minutes

The solution to the sea-of-toys-on-the-floor problem is to make it just as easy (or easier) for kids to put things away as it is to take them out. Books can be yanked off shelves a lot more quickly than they can be put back, and clothes can be pulled out of drawers more easily than they can be folded and put away. And kids don't mind a mess, so you probably won't find your children implementing new organizational systems on their own. Instead, this job is left to you. Start by picking up a few topless baskets and bins. Most kids won't bother lifting a lid or cover to put something away, but they will drop or toss a toy into a container with no top.

Thursday: Play the Label Game

⏱ 20 minutes

While labels don't belong everywhere in your home, they can be extremely useful—and even fun!—in your kids' rooms. Use a label maker or your computer printer to create some simple graphic labels that will help your kids identify where things go. Pictures of blocks, Legos, art supplies, or dolls will help them remember where things go and encourage them to put them away when they're done. Play the Match the Label game and give kids an incentive to clean up after themselves. You'll see the mess disappear in no time.

Friday: Stack It Up

🕒 20 minutes

Okay, so plastic stackable drawers aren't much of an interior design statement. Luckily, the apples of your eye don't give a hoot about that. In kids' rooms, function takes precedence over form, so invest in some sturdy stackable drawers and cubbies that the kids can use for easy storage. Clear plastic allows you to see what's being stored inside, and cubbies work well for items that can be on display, such as stuffed animals or dolls. Just remember to only stack drawers and cubbies as high as kids can reach. Otherwise, they'll have a legitimate excuse when things end up all over the floor, and they could get hurt trying to get to something.

Saturday: Play Some Hoops

🕒 30 minutes

Here's a great idea your kids won't be able to resist. Go to your local sporting goods store and pick up a small, wall-mountable basketball hoop and a plush ball for inside play. When you get home, install the hoop above the kids' hamper or wastepaper basket to make gathering dirty clothes or throwing away trash a little more fun. The kids will be consumed by the competition to see who can make the most baskets, and you'll be satisfied to see all those socks and crumpled pieces of paper leave the floor. It's a win-win!

Sunday: Save Space with Bunk Beds

🕐 30 minutes

When you think of bunk beds you may flash back to memories of sleeping in an ant-infested lean-to at summer camp or a cramped dorm room in college. These might not be positive associations for an adult who's moved on to bigger and better, but most kids think bunk beds are awesome. This is the beauty of youth: The novelty of climbing a ladder to get into bed still has the ability to thrill and excite. If your kids share a room and space is at a premium (a common cause of clutter), bunk beds may just be the perfect solution for everyone. Then it's just a matter of deciding who gets the top.

Kids' Rooms Week 2

Monday: Play Hide-and-Seek

🕐 20 minutes

Many of the principles you apply to other parts of your home can also be put to work in your kids' rooms. One of these is the "If you can't see it, that's good enough" strategy. In other areas of life, hiding things is not a terrific idea. But in home organization, it's what it's all about. For example, you might want to pick up a few flat, rectangular storage bins on wheels that your kids can use for under-the-bed storage. You could also hang a curtain in front of the closet so clothes, shoes, and toys are easily accessible but not visible. Also, consider using a screen or room divider to section off the sleeping and play areas of the room.

Tuesday: Put the Toys to Bed

🕐 **10 minutes**

Do the dolls and stuffed animals in your kids' rooms seem to be multiplying? Keep them in check before they start a mutiny and take over the house! Here's an idea: a toy hammock. It's essentially a miniature hammock, usually made of nylon netting, which gives dolls and plush toys a place other than the floor to hang out. You can either loop the ends of the hammock around bedposts or hang the hammock on hooks in a corner of the room. When your kids get ready for bed at night, tell them that their toys need to "go to sleep," too. This will make an end-of-the-day cleanup part of the evening routine.

Wednesday: Get Creative with Clothing Storage

🕐 **30 minutes**

When it comes to organization in the kids' rooms, you have to make it as easy as possible if you want them to participate. So in terms of clothing, the traditional storage rules may not apply. Younger kids might struggle with hangers and dresser drawers, so you need an easier alternative. A couple of ideas include bins and cubbies, whose open-front or open-top designs make it easy for kids to both remove items and put them away. Bins and cubbies both come in stackable styles and on wheels, so you can store them in a closet, under the bed, or anywhere that they'll be easily accessible but out of the way.

Thursday: Reuse Containers

🕐 10 minutes

Kids have lots of little items in their rooms—dominos, army men, and marbles—that can easily get scattered all over the floor. To keep small items together and organized, put them in empty peanut butter jars, juice bottles, yogurt cups, and any other washable food containers you have in the house. Make sure only to use plastic (never glass), and try to use clear plastic so kids can see what's inside. If you don't have clear plastic containers, simply label the container. If possible use containers that can't be recycled, and you'll help keep trash out of the landfill.

Friday: Use Those Extra Shoelaces

🕐 10 minutes

When you buy new shoes, they sometimes come with extra shoelaces. This is great, but how often do you actually use the extras? After a while (and a couple of kids), you can end up with quite the shoelace collection. Instead of throwing them away or stuffing them in a drawer, never to be heard from again, put those laces to good use. Hang them on the wall of the kids' rooms and snap hairclips onto them for visible storage, or use them to hang framed artwork or photos for a fun, homemade look. You can also use them as sporty ponytail holders or bracelets. There's no end to the possibilities!

Saturday: Try Carpet Tiles

🕐 25 minutes

Kids and fancy home furnishings do not mix, and for this reason we strongly advise you not to give each of your children his or her own Persian rug. A better idea would be individual carpet tiles, such as Flor brand, which can be joined together to fit the shape and size of any room. Carpet tiles are especially great for kids' rooms because if the carpet gets damaged, you can simply replace the damaged tile instead of buying a whole new rug. Carpet tiles can also help protect your gorgeous hardwood floors from the spills, scuffs, and scratches of childhood. The tiles are held in place by an adhesive on the back side, so once your kids are grown, just pull them up to give the room a more adult feel. Kids can choose from a wide variety of patterns and designs and can lay down the tiles themselves—it's that easy!

Almost Perfect

To clean your floors, invest in a couple of different mopheads: one for wood floors (use Murphy Oil Soap to make your wood floors shine) and one for kitchen cleaners.

Sunday: Make Cleanup a Part of the Day

🕐 30 minutes

The notion of cause and effect is generally lost on little ones. Their room starts out clean, your kids play for an hour, and before they know it, it's messy again. The mess likely bothers you much more than it bothers them, so you need to find a way to incorporate cleanup into their regular daily routine. For example, Good Morning Cleanup might include straightening the bedding, pulling up the shades, and putting yesterday's clothes in the hamper. Nighttime Cleanup can precede getting ready for bed and include putting the day's toys back in their containers, pulling down the shades, and choosing an outfit for the next day.

Kids' Rooms Week 3

Monday: Go with the Theme

🕐 20 minutes

Many kids' rooms have themes, such as Under the Sea or Jungle. A great way to create more storage space in a bedroom is to incorporate it into your child's theme. For example, if your daughter loves flowers, use gardening objects, like flower pots and planters, for storage. If your son's room has a pirate theme, use fishing nets to hold toys and a trunk (or "treasure chest") to hold blankets and pillows. Let your kids lead this project, as they might be the ones to come up with the most creative ideas.

Tuesday: Steal from Other Rooms

🕐 15 minutes

Some of the best storage items for kids' rooms can actually be found in the home office or the kitchen. For instance, shallow metal or plastic trays like those you use for outgoing mail in your home office work great for keeping kids' homework and artwork in order. In a baby's room, these trays are great for storing folded onesies and socks and keeping them within easy reach. Likewise, the hanging mesh baskets you use for produce in your kitchen are great for holding small toys or hair accessories. Just make sure to hang the baskets at a reachable height and to let kids know that yanking on them or trying to hang from them is a strict no-no.

Wednesday: Trashcans Aren't Just for Garbage

🕐 10 minutes

You'd probably love to see half your kids' toys go into the garbage, wouldn't you? Now you can! Pick up a few small, colorful trashcans to be used for storage in your kids' rooms. These can be used to organize toys, sports equipment, craft supplies, and any number of other items that are currently roaming freely. When the cans are empty, they can be stacked and kept out of the way. Trashcans with handle cutouts can be hung on the wall to free up even more floor space and add some visual interest to the room.

Almost Perfect

Wooden fruit and vegetable boxes make terrific storage containers for toys and shoes. Just lightly sand them so the kids won't get splinters, and if you'd like, add a coat of paint or stain to match the décor of the room. These boxes can sit on the floor, hang on the wall, or be stacked and used like shelving.

Thursday: Store and Swap

🕐 15 minutes

If your kids have an overabundance of toys (aka more than they can possibly play with in a lifetime), give the ol' store-and-swap method a try. With your child's help, weed out the toys that he or she isn't that into at the moment. These might be seasonal toys or those that have simply been pushed aside to make way for the newer ones. Store these in a large lidded plastic container and put the collection away in the closet or slide it under the bed. Then on a rainy day a few months later, bring the box back out, swapping the stored toys for other playthings that have lost their savor. Your children will have regained their interest in the stored toys, and they won't have been clogging up space in the meantime.

Friday: Sweep It Up

🕐 10 minutes

On days when the multipiece toys like Legos, dominos, and marbles come out, the floor of your child's room can become completely obscured by teeny toys and plastic pieces. A great way to get all these pieces into a pile for easier pickup is to sweep them up with a broom. Pick up a child-size broom and dustpan from the toy store and then teach your child how to sweep up toys and dump them back into their proper bin or storage container. This will take far less time than picking up each individual piece by hand, and it'll make your child feel like an adult to use a broom just like Mommy and Daddy.

Saturday: Double-Duty Dish Bins

🕐 15 minutes

Those plastic dish bins with the rounded corners aren't only good for washing dishes; they also make fantastic storage containers for your kids' rooms. Let your kids choose a couple of bins in their favorite colors, and then help them choose items to store in them. Great candidates include blocks, Legos, action figures, and craft supplies. For small children, you might consider labeling the outside of the bin with a photo or illustration of what should go inside. Then it's just a matter of matching the item to the image to put it away!

Sunday: Keep the Crib

🕐 10 minutes

When babies grow out of their cribs and move into "big kid" beds, the parents will typically sell the crib or hand it down to a family member. While this is a fine option, there's also another way to use a crib after your child has grown out of it: as storage! A crib makes a great storage bin for stuffed animals and other toys, pillows and blankets, and any other big or bulky items that don't quite fit anywhere else. If you want your kids to be able to access the items on their own, place a stepstool next to the crib or lower one side so they can reach in. And as with all storage bins, make sure to tell your kids that their toys have to go back in the crib at the end of the day. Most kids will love putting their dolls and stuffed animals to bed at night.

Kids' Rooms Week 4

Monday: Cast a Net for Sports Balls

🕐 20 minutes

Most kids have an array of balls they play with, from tennis balls and basketballs to kick balls and footballs. Because of their awkward shape, sports balls are difficult to store, and this is why your little ones need a ball net for their room. You can buy these at toy and sporting goods stores, or use a piece of fishnet or utility netting you already have. Just fill the net with balls and gather it at the top with a rope or bungee cord and hang it from a solidly installed hook. This way, the kids' sports balls will be out from underfoot but still within reach.

Tuesday: Turn Your Kid into a Do-Gooder

🕐 20 minutes

When clutter gets to be too much, it's time to purge some items. In the case of your kids' belongings, they will likely be loathe to let things go, even if they haven't played with them for months. The "That's mine!" mentality is just how kids roll. A good way to clear out clutter and teach your child to spread the wealth is to introduce her to the wide world of charitable donations. Before her birthday or a holiday, ask your child to choose five toys that she would like to give to a child in need. If the idea of donating isn't inspiring enough on its own, explain to your child that she needs to give away some old toys before she can receive any new ones. Then take her with you when you make the donation—to a church or hospital, perhaps—so she can see the effect her generosity can have on others.

Wednesday: Lower the Bar

🕐 15 minutes

Do you wonder why all your child's clothes are in a heap on the floor of the closet? Take a look at the bar where those clothes should be hanging. If it's up at adult level and your child is still young, that could be your answer. An easy fix for this problem is to install a bar a foot or two lower, where your child can reach it. Buy a spring-loaded bar that will fit in any size space automatically. Once the bar is in, show your child how to take down clothes and hang them back up again.

Thursday: Put Safety First

🕐 20 minutes

Depending on your children's ages, you may want to store items requiring supervision either out of reach or in locked containers. The last thing you need is to walk in their room one day and find that they've eaten a box of crayons or glued their fingers together. Set up a system where your kids have to ask you to retrieve certain items, such as art materials like paints and glues, anything sharp like scissors or staplers, or items requiring electricity. Of course, your kids will try to get to these items on their own anyway, so take extra precautions. If you have tall shelves, anchor them to the wall so they can't fall over. Also, store heavy items on bottom shelves where they can't fall and crush any little bodies.

Friday: Make Their Rooms Spillproof

🕐 10 minutes

Kids are notorious spillers. From grape juice to spaghetti sauce, no carpet is safe when a child is near. Chances are that spaghetti sauce won't ever find its way into your child's room, but a cup of juice very well might. Today is your chance to say no to spills; remember, prevention should always be part of the solution. If your kids have a rug in their room, now is the time to Scotchgard it. It will take twenty-four hours to dry thoroughly, so have your kids sleep on an air mattress or in the guest bedroom. They'll love the chance to have a Friday night adventure.

Saturday: Make Bracelet Tubes

🕐 20 minutes

Recycling is generally the way to go when it comes to cardboard paper towel tubes, but you can also use running out of paper towels as a craft opportunity for the kids. Sit down at a table with a few empty toilet paper and paper towel tubes and some markers, crayons, stickers, and other art supplies. Have each child decorate her own tube for use as a bracelet, watch, or hair elastic holder. This will not only keep the kids busy for a little while (Amen to that), but it will also keep bracelets, watches, and hair elastics from scattering all over the room.

Sunday: Save Those Newspapers

🕐 10 minutes

Newspapers are another item that generally goes in the recycling bin when you're done with them but they can have a second life in your kids' rooms. Whenever the kids are planning to color, make crafts, or perform some other messy activity, spread out a layer of newspaper first. You probably want to make it two or three sheets thick, just in case of a spill. This way, when and if a cup of paint gets overturned or a glue bottle starts leaking, the newspaper will catch it instead of the floor or carpet. When craft time is over, simply gather up the newspaper and throw it away. Or better yet, have your kids do it. If cleanup is that easy, they should be ready and willing to do their part.

Kids' Rooms Week 5

Monday: Fill Up a Beach Bucket

🕐 10 minutes

If you live near a lake or the ocean, you probably take your kids on frequent trips to the beach in the summertime. All parents of water babies know how much stuff a beach day involves, and they also know how annoying it can be to arrive and realize you forgot something. Here's a fun way to simplify: Take a big plastic beach bucket and fill it with all the items you need for a day at the beach, from sunglasses and sunscreen to plastic shovels and beach towels. The kids' might enjoy having their own personal beach buckets filled with items they've chosen. When you're ready to go, just put the buckets in the trunk of the car and hit the road!

Tuesday: Go with the Faux

🕐 10 minutes

Throughout this book we recommend that you add potted plants or vases of fresh flowers to your rooms to bring some color and life to your decorating schemes. This advice also goes for the kids' rooms but with a slight difference. A live plant or a decorative vase of flowers is just too much responsibility for most kids, so we heartily recommend the fake variety as an alternative. Go on a little expedition to your local craft store and let each child choose a plant or bunch of flowers for his or her room. If it gets knocked over during an impromptu pillow fight, there'll be no mess to clean up.

Wednesday: Hide the Evidence

🕒 10 minutes

The space under the bed is one of those classic clutter repositories. While you've probably been able to wrestle your own under-the-bed storage into some kind of order, kids are just not as motivated to keep this area neat. On the contrary, this is where things get shoved when you tell them to clean their rooms. Kids are all about appearances, not thoroughness. They consider the spaces under their beds the perfect spots to hide balled-up dirty clothes and sneakers, old homework assignments, and empty juice cups. You can try to fight city hall on this one, but you will not win. A better plan is to hide the evidence with a dust ruffle. We made this recommendation for your own bedroom, too, but it will be even more useful in the kids' rooms. With kids, sometimes out of sight out of mind is good enough.

Thursday: Banish Winter

🕒 10 minutes

Kids are small, but their winter clothes can be bulky and difficult to store. We're talking about puffy winter coats, thick wool sweaters, snow pants, hats, scarves, gloves, boots, and anything else meant to prevent frostbite. When spring rolls around, it's time to put this stuff into storage. But how? Your kids' winter wardrobe can easily fill a closet, and you might not have the space to spare. Take all smaller, soft items— including scarves, hats, mittens, and gloves—and shove them in the arms of the coats. Coats can still be hung, but now you'll have fewer items to find space for. And when winter returns, you won't have to wonder, "Now where did I put those gloves?"

Almost Perfect

Another option for storing bulky clothing items is reusable vacuum-seal pouches. These are basically durable plastic bags with one-way air valves. You fill a bag with your fluffiest clothing, seal it, and then use a small vacuum-like device to remove the air. This can shrink items to half their size or smaller! Vacuum sealers come in various sizes and styles and can be found at most home goods and hardware stores.

Friday: Put Toys to Work

🕐 15 minutes

If your kids are into construction equipment and have a bunch of toy replicas in their rooms, why not put them to work? Teach your kids how machines like dump trucks and backhoes work on real-world construction sites, and then challenge them to try some similar tasks in their own rooms. For example, can their toy dump truck pick up the Legos they just finished playing with and transport them to their storage container on the other side of the room? How about the craft supplies strewn all over the floor? When they're done, remind them to "park" their construction vehicles in a proper place, too.

Saturday: Look But Don't Touch

🕒 10 minutes

Kids are clumsy, especially little ones. This is why we make them sit down before they hold their baby sisters and brothers. Similarly, it's wise to keep breakable items, heirlooms, and fragile art pieces out of their reach. This doesn't mean you can't display them in the kids' rooms, though the most valuable items would probably be safer elsewhere. For those you feel comfortable keeping in the kids' space, such as their own art work or framed photographs, place them on high shelves where they can be seen but not touched. If the shelves are high enough, this will also protect the items from a ball that comes flying across the room (a common occurrence, surely).

Sunday: Think Outside the Bookshelf

🕒 15 minutes

In other parts of a house, a bookshelf with anything on it besides books and maybe a few small decorative items can begin to look cluttered. In a child's room, though, dolls, stuffed animals, and other small toys are fun additions that display the child's personality. And if these toys are on a shelf, that also means they're not on the floor. A small bookshelf also makes a great bedside table in a kid's room. This way, your child can read before bed—and reach her favorite snuggle buddy, Mr. Teddy—without getting out from under the covers.

FROM DETERGENT TO DRYER SHEETS: THE LAUNDRY ROOM

Of all the rooms in your home, the laundry room is probably the one you worry about least. That's good. Your washing machine and ironing board aren't crying themselves to sleep at night due to neglect. But, it's in your best interest to give this room a little attention. If your washer and dryer are hidden beneath heaps of clothing, or if the floor is littered with mostly empty bottles of detergent and stain remover, doing laundry will feel like more of a chore than it really is. You want to be able to get in, get out, and get on with something fun—and some easy organization is just the way to do it.

Monday: Toss Those Empties

🕐 **10 minutes**

This task is about getting rid of all those mostly empty detergent jugs, stain remover spray bottles, stain sticks, dryer sheet boxes, and any other garbage that's currently clogging up your laundry room. You'll never get those last few drops of detergent out of the jug, so give it up! If you have two half-full containers of the same kind of detergent, pour one into the other and toss the empty one. Recycle any recyclable items and throw the rest in the trash.

Tuesday: Arrange According to Use

🕐 **15 minutes**

An easy way to prevent your laundry room from turning into a hell hole is to arrange products and supplies according to how often you use them. Keep anything you use on a regular basis within easy reach, such as in an open-front cabinet or an easily accessible drawer. Store small supplies that you need to grab quickly, such as stain sticks and sprays, in an open bin. Extras and specialty items, like bleach or detergent made specifically for black garments, can be kept higher up or in the back of a cabinet where they'll be out of the way. This will prevent you from having to pull everything off the shelf to find what you're looking for.

Wednesday: Sort the Smart Way

⏱ 20 minutes

Staring at that mountain of laundry with fear in your eyes? Don't fret; this is going to be a snap! All you need is a sorting system: a hamper, bin, or rolling cart with three different sections. Once you have that in place, go through the pile and separate whites, colors, and delicate items. Once you have everything sorted you can start doing loads. Whites should be washed in hot water, possibly with a little bleach to get them brighter; colors should be washed in cold water to prevent colors from running; and delicates should be done by hand in the sink or in the washer on a delicates setting. Check the tags for washing instructions if you still have questions.

Almost Perfect

It's tempting to just dump bleach on top of your clothes before you start the washer. Trust us, you won't be happy when the bleach eats a hole clean through your favorite shirt. To prevent this tragedy, only add bleach to a white wash after the washer has filled with water but before the agitator starts moving. This will dilute the bleach, allowing it to do its job—while you go enjoy your life.

Thursday: Do Your Laundry *and* a Good Deed

⏱ 10 minutes

In addition to a regular hamper or sorting bin for dirty clothes, keep a "charity bag" in your laundry room. That way, when an unwanted item comes out of the dryer, it can go right into the bag instead of back up to your bedroom where it will languish for a few more months. A simple linen drawstring bag will do, and you can hang it on a hook near the washer and dryer. When the bag's full, bring it to the local Salvation Army, Goodwill, or other charity organization that accepts clothing donations; some charities will even pick up. The loss of your unwanted garments will be someone else's gain!

Friday: Let It Dry

🕐 20 minutes

You probably know (and may have learned the hard way) that certain garments should not go in the dryer. These include delicate items like underwire bras and silk and lace lingerie, and anything made of cotton or wool that you don't want to shrink, such as shirts or sweaters. When you take these items out of the washing machine, move them immediately to a drying rack or flat surface where they can air-dry. Today, buy a collapsible wood or plastic drying rack—you can simply fold it up and store it when not in use. For garments like sweaters that need to retain their shape, buy a breathable mesh drying rack. These look like little trampolines for your clothes and can be stacked to handle more than one item at a time.

Saturday: Put the Iron in Its Place

🕐 15 minutes

The ironing board and iron are awkwardly shaped items that don't really "go" anywhere. When the ironing board is open it takes up lots of space, and when the iron is hot it's hard to put it away. Luckily, these two problems have simple solutions that you can implement in a matter of minutes. Go to your local home goods store and pick up a wall-mounted, all-in-one iron and ironing board holder. This handy-dandy item consists of a heat-resistant slot for the iron and a hook from which you can hang the collapsed ironing board. Choose a spot on the wall for the holder and never trip over the iron cord or the ironing board again!

Sunday: Put up a Clothesline

🕐 25 minutes

We know this isn't *Little House on the Prairie*, but before you judge clotheslines as being outdated, consider the benefits. You'll save money on electric bills and dryer sheets; clothes dried in the fresh air have a crisp, clean scent that only Mother Nature can provide; and sunshine kills bacteria and gets your whites whiter the natural way. Also, a clothesline isn't just a string between two trees anymore. There are all kinds of easy-to-use modern styles, such as a single-pole rotary clothesline, which folds up like an umbrella, or a mounted clothes line, which can be installed on the wall of a patio. A retractable clothes line for above your bathtub is another option, and there are even "soft touch" clothespins that won't leave ugly dents in fabric.

Laundry Room Week 2

Monday: Fold on the Spot

🕐 10 minutes

You know the drill: You take clothes out of the dryer, toss them into a laundry basket, and promptly forget about them. There they sit for days on end, becoming more and more of a scattered mess as each family member goes rummaging for his or her garments. This is not a good plan. Instead, create a workspace in your laundry room so you can fold clothes right out of the dryer. Any countertop or table will do. This way, clothes won't sit and get wrinkly (which will in turn cut your ironing load), and you'll decrease the chances of a sock or pair of underwear going AWOL.

Tuesday: Scale Down

🕐 15 minutes

Is there not enough space for an ironing station in your laundry room? Go pick up a portable tabletop ironing board or one that's built into a cabinet that can be mounted on the wall. With the latter, you just open the cabinet door and the ironing board swivels out, set up and ready to go. Also look at travel irons, which are about half to two-thirds the size of a regular iron and are available with retractable cords. When you're not using the iron, it'll be easy to store it out of sight.

Almost Perfect

The average person spends five to seven hours a week in the laundry room. Hard to believe, right? If you're spending a significant chunk of your life doing laundry, make it easy on yourself. Don't be afraid to throw something in the wash and go out for a while. Having fun with your family is better than laundry any day.

Wednesday: Go Dirty

🕐 5 minutes

If the laundry volume is out of control in your house, you might be washing clothes and linens before their time. Modern washers and dryers are so easy to use that people sometimes get overzealous on laundry day and wash items that don't need it yet, such as sheets that have only been on the bed for a week or jackets that have only been worn once or twice. We're not suggesting you abandon personal hygiene, but think about what you wash when. You could save yourself three to five loads of laundry a month (and a boatload in electricity bills) if you leave those sheets on the bed for another week or wear that jacket one more time before washing.

Thursday: Let There Be Light

🕐 15 minutes

Check out the lighting in your laundry room. Is it too harsh or too dim? What you want is adequate lighting that isn't over-bearing. You won't be spending as much time in here as you do in your home office (hopefully), but you'll spend enough that the mood of the room matters. Ideally, your laundry area will be inviting and warm so that you'll actually want to spend time there. Changing the lighting doesn't have to cost much, either. Sometimes the simple addition of a floor lamp that glows instead of glares can completely transform the feel of the room.

Friday: Make It Pretty

🕐 20 minutes

Yes, we're still talking about the laundry room. Who said that a laundry area has to be ugly? If yours is in the basement or another part of your home that does not receive much natural light, consider painting the walls a cheery color. Hang artwork or photographs that you enjoy looking at near your washer and dryer. These small touches can increase the human element of a space that is more typically dominated by machines. Also consider picking up a few attractive baskets that can be useful for keeping detergents and fabric softeners in order. These will add some texture and visual appeal to the space.

Saturday: Think of Laundry Day While Shopping

🕐 **20 minutes**

When shopping for clothes, don't just consider the aesthetic appeal of an item. Think also about the effort involved in cleaning it. In certain professions, a dry-clean-only suit may be required, but for those who have the opportunity to dress more casually, just not buying dry-clean-only items can reduce the hassle and cost of maintaining your clothes. Also, if you have dry-clean items now that you're not wearing because washing them is too much trouble, get them ready to donate. You don't need clothes—even beautiful ones—hanging around if you're not wearing them.

Sunday: Go Full Steam Ahead

🕐 **20 minutes**

If you're in a hurry to get to an event but don't have time to iron your outfit (Gee, how often does that happen?), try this trick: Hang your garment in the bathroom and keep the door closed while you take a nice, hot shower. The steam from the hot water will naturally relax the wrinkles right out of your clothes, eliminating one step of preparation. If the wrinkles haven't completely disappeared by the end of your shower, just leave the garment in the bathroom with the door closed for an extra few minutes.

Laundry Room Week 3

Monday: Keep Sheets Together

🕐 10 minutes

Do you ever find yourself turning the house inside out searching for a misplaced pillowcase? Do you sometimes resort to making your bed with a fitted sheet from one set and a flat sheet from another? When clean sheets come out of the dryer, fold the entire set except for one pillowcase. Then, slide the stack of folded sheets inside the pillowcase. Stack sets neatly in your linen closet and you'll always be able to grab an entire matching set when you need it.

Tuesday: Treat That Stain, STAT

🕐 15 minutes

Stains on clothing are just a fact of life, especially with kids. But this doesn't mean you have to bid farewell to every garment you spill on. For most stains, there is an easy treatment that will get it out or at least prepare it for a run through the washing machine. For oily stains, make a paste of sugar and water and rub it into the stain before washing. For nonoily stains, mix together 1 pint lukewarm water, 1 teaspoon liquid detergent, and 1 teaspoon white vinegar. Apply to the stain until it disappears and then rinse with water. For ink stains, soak with hairspray and let dry, and then brush lightly with a solution of white vinegar and water. For wine and fruit juice spills, make a paste of lemon juice and salt. Let this mixture sit on the stain for thirty minutes before laundering the garment.

> ## *Almost Perfect*
>
> Afraid you won't be able to remember stain remedies when it really counts? Post a cheat sheet of them somewhere in your laundry room where you can see it. Also keep some of the items commonly used to treat stains (salt, white vinegar, lemon juice) on hand right in your laundry room so you don't have to go running all over the house to get them.

Wednesday: Use Powder Detergent

🕒 5 minutes

If you use powder laundry detergent, you know of the benefits over the liquid variety. It's cheaper, you go through it less quickly, and spills are not so catastrophic. However, the packaging for powder detergents is not typically all that user friendly. It generally comes in boxes, with a perforated tab to pour out of, which can create a mess when you try to pour it into a measuring cup. Here's a better idea: Get a plastic container—a lidded food storage container or plastic canister will work well—and transfer the powder detergent into it. Then drop a measuring cup in the container and you're good to go.

Thursday: Fold to a Beat

🕒 15 minutes

The laundry room is not the most exciting place to be. You pretty much go in there to put in loads of laundry, fold them when they're done, and possibly iron a few garments. Make it a little more fun by adding some tunes. A portable CD player, radio, or MP3 player won't take up too much space but will go a long way toward making laundry day a bit more interesting. Rock out to your favorite oldies or catch up on the latest news. There's no reason why you can't multitask!

Friday: Create a Laundry Lost and Found

🕐 10 minutes

If you're the lucky person in charge of your household's laundry, you probably feel like a bit of a treasure hunter. From loose change and packs of gum to wadded-up cash and hairclips, you must find all kinds of things in the pockets of your family's clothing. Place these items in a lost-and-found bin near your washer and dryer. Toss in anything you find in pockets or at the bottom of the dryer, and then once a week do a show and tell so everyone can claim their lost items. Also ask everyone to check their pockets *before* putting clothes in the hamper. While things like buttons will go through the wash unharmed, items like lip gloss and tissues can break apart and get all over everything.

Saturday: Forget the Sink

🕐 10 minutes

Ideally, a laundry room will be outfitted with a big utility sink where you can rinse out or soak especially grimy or stained garments before they go into the washing machine. However, we can't all have such luxury. If you're one of the unlucky sinkless folk, go into your kitchen and find a big plastic bowl or bucket that will do the job just as well. Fill it with water and keep it in the laundry room, being sure to empty it and fill it with fresh water on a regular basis. If you feel funny about having an open container of liquid sitting in your laundry room, choose a container with a lid instead. That way if you accidentally kick it over, you won't find yourself in the middle of a flood.

Sunday: Iron with Care

🕐 **30 minutes**

Everyone's experienced or at least heard of this disaster: You're in a hurry, getting ready for a wedding or some other big event, and while attempting to iron your new silk dress you burn a big hole right through it. To cut back on the rush, and on the big pile of clothes that need to be ironed that's likely sitting in your laundry room right now, take the time to get your ironing out of the way today. It won't take as long as you think, and once it's done, it's done—until next time. Always follow the ironing instructions on an item's tag to get the right setting and temperature.

Laundry Room Week 4

Monday: Install a Bar

🕐 **10 minutes**

No, we're not advising you to bring alcohol into your laundry room—even though that would make laundry more fun. Instead we suggest that you install a bar for hanging clothes. A spring-loaded suspension bar can fit between two walls in a narrow space or between a cabinet and the wall. This will make it easy for you to hang up clothes once they've been ironed or to hang-dry certain garments, such as bras and pantyhose, that don't take up much space. Measure the space before you go to the store to buy the bar, and once it's hung up, make sure it's secure. The last thing you need is for a bar full of hanging clothes to fall on your head.

Tuesday: Make It Multipurpose

🕐 20 minutes

If you're one of the lucky few with a really spacious laundry room in your home, you might consider using it to store items that aren't laundry related. This is not an invitation to hoard more clutter, but there are lots of odds and ends that can find a good home in your laundry room. Examples include holiday decorations, gift wrap, craft supplies, and sporting equipment—all organized in labeled bins, of course. Keep any storage separate from the laundry area by placing it on a separate shelving unit or sectioning off the room with a room divider.

Wednesday: Conceal with Curtains

🕐 20 minutes

If your laundry facilities are in a common area, such as the living room or kitchen, you might want to disguise its appearance somehow. We're not calling your washing machine ugly, but chances are it doesn't exactly go with your décor. Here's an easy project you can do in a matter of minutes: Take a spring-loaded suspension bar that will fit in front of your washer and dryer and select a couple of curtain panels to hang from it.

You can hang the bar high and get long curtains to disguise the whole area, or you can choose to keep it the exact height of the washer and dryer. Either way, just keep the curtains closed when you're not using the laundry facilities and simply slide them open when you have to get in there.

Thursday: Stash a Sewing Kit

🕒 15 minutes

The laundry room is probably the place where you'll first discover holes, missing buttons, and other issues with your clothing, which makes it the perfect place to keep a sewing kit! It doesn't have to be elaborate, and you don't have to be Martha Stewart to make use of it. Just a few spools of thread (brown, black, and a couple of favorite colors), a few needles, and a pair of scissors are all you really need to quickly stitch up a hole or restore an errant button to its rightful place before throwing it in the wash. For the more motivated among us, and for those with a little more space to work with, you might consider setting up a small sewing station in the laundry room with a sewing machine and other supplies.

Friday: Take a Seat

🕐 10 minutes

Spending a lot of time on your feet isn't good for you. You may notice pain in your feet or an ache in your lower back after you've stood and folded laundry even a half-hour. To remedy this problem, take a seat! Bring a chair into the laundry room and place it next to a surface you can use for folding. A folding chair would be perfect, as you could simply fold and stow it when not in use. Your laundry room doesn't need more clutter, but your body deserves a break.

Saturday: Dust Those Machines

🕐 10 minutes

It may seem ironic to have to clean machines that are made specifically for cleaning, but the truth is even washing machines get dusty from time to time, and dryers can become speckled with lint from your laundry. This isn't a chore you have to do often, but every once in a while, when things are looking particularly hairy, dampen a rag or dish cloth that is already in the dirty pile and use it to wipe off the top, side, and front of your washing machine and dryer. When you're done, just toss the rag or cloth in with the next load of laundry.

Sunday: Keep a Trashcan Nearby

🕐 5 minutes

You may not immediately think of the laundry room as a place in your home that needs its own trashcan, but it definitely does. In order to keep your dryer in good working order, you'll have to clean the lint trap often. You'll also find things like tissues and gum wrappers in the pockets of people's pants and jackets. Additionally there are things like laundry detergent bottles and used fabric softener sheets that need to be thrown away. Keep the trashcan lined with a plastic bag to make emptying it a snap, and you might even consider keeping a small recycling bin here for recyclable detergent jugs and stain remover spray bottles.

Laundry Room Week 5

Monday: Train That Stain Stick

🕐 **5 minutes**

We're not suggesting you're clumsy, but if you don't already own a pen-size Tide To Go stain stick, go to your nearest store and pick one (or several) up. This tiny tool is indispensable when it comes to stain removal. If you carry one with you at all times—in your purse, the glove compartment of your car, even your coat pocket—then you will virtually eliminate the need for stain sticks and sprays in your laundry room. This will not only cut down on clutter, but it will also increase the chances that stains will come out in the wash. The earlier a stain is treated, the better!

Almost Perfect

To get soft towels use a good fabric softener. This does a better job than the sheets. However, if you're worried about flyaway hair or static cling, the sheets will do the trick.

Tuesday: X Marks the Sock

🕐 10 minutes

Lost socks are a laundry room cliché that you don't want to per-petuate. When you wash socks, put them in a durable mesh lin-gerie bag. Normally these are used for bras and other delicates, but they also work great for keeping single socks from drifting away from their mates. When you move the clothes from the washer to the dryer, remove the socks from the bag. If you still lose socks after using this method, you can safely assume that your dryer is eating them for breakfast.

Wednesday: Shrink It

🕐 20 minutes

If you have a garment that's too big on you, you may think your only option is to give it away. Not so! Depending on the material, you may be able to shrink the item down to the right size. Cotton items, for example, can be shrunk in hot water and then dried on high in the dryer. Say you want to shrink a denim jacket. You can either run it through a hot wash by itself or with other color items you want to try to shrink, or you can dip it in a tub of very hot water. It's not important that the garment is still hot or even wet when it goes in the dryer; it just has to have been dunked in hot water. Then dry the jacket on high and see if it fits. If it's still too big (or now too small), you can still donate it as you originally planned.

Thursday: Be More Disposable

🕐 10 minutes

A canister of disposable wet wipes or baby wipes is a great thing to keep in most rooms of the house, but it's especially handy in the laundry room. These wipes are perfect for wiping up detergent spills, clearing away dust, or snatching floating balls of lint that have fallen out of the dryer. Keep the wipes in a cabinet where you can easily reach them, and just toss the used wipes in the trash when you're done using them.

Friday: Wash More

🕐 20 minutes

Washers and dryers are made for clothes and linens, but depending on the type of washer and dryer you have, you may be able to launder other items. These might include duffel bags, baseball caps, and even smelly sneakers. Canvas bags wash very well in regular washing machines but will likely shrink up a bit in the dryer. Baseball caps should be washed on the gentle cycle and air-dried so they keep their shape. And sneakers can be washed in cold water but should also air-dry, as any rubber or foam components could melt in high heat.

Almost Perfect

Use a vinegar (or lemon) and water mix to clean out your washing machine; just drop some in like it's laundry detergent and run a cycle. The acid in these mixes takes care of buildup caused by hard water.

Saturday: Store Seasonal Items

🕐 20 minutes

We don't want to encourage you to stockpile junk in your laundry room, but there are certain items that it just makes sense to store here—but only if you have the room. One example is seasonal clothing and shoes. Seasonal clothing to store in the laundry room could include winter gear such as coats, snow pants, hats, gloves, and scarves, and summer gear such as bathing suits, shorts, tank tops, and light pajamas. Winter footwear might include boots and heavy socks, and for summer, flip-flops and sandals. Because these are all in the laundry "family," you'll logically remember that you're keeping them here.

Sunday: Add Luggage

🕐 20 minutes

If you're using your laundry room to store off-season clothes, (see "Store Seasonal Items") pack them away using suitcases and other pieces of luggage. By storing two items in the space of one, you effectively kill two birds with one stone. Also, luggage is a logical spot to store clothing, so when it's time to retrieve your seasonal clothing items, you won't have to think too hard about where they are. Also, vacations generally coincide with the retrieval of seasonal garments, so you might not even have much to pack for your trips!

GOING DOWN UNDER:
THE BASEMENT

If you have a case of the basement blues, it could be because you've taken an out-of-sight, out-of-mind approach to clearing your clutter. You move stuff down but never out. And out—by the curb—is probably where a lot of it belongs. Basements are an easy place to let things get out of hand, and some of the tidiest homes have disorganized disasters lurking beneath their floorboards. Time to clean out your house's dirty little secret.

Monday: Clear a Path

🕐 15 minutes

The first thing you need to do is to give yourself some elbow-room to work. Scan the basement and set your priorities on eliminating the most obvious, aisle-jamming items: the ancient ice skates, the large picture frame with the cracked glass you've been meaning to replace, the broken air conditioner you trip over at every turn. Moving them to the side to create aisles isn't good enough. Sort items into three piles: Keep, Donate, and Toss. You're likely to find some sentimental items down there, and those are okay to keep. But the broken lamp you bought at a garage sale ten years ago and still don't know how to fix? Adios.

Tuesday: Keep It

🕐 20 minutes

When you find things you want to keep, find a way to store it correctly. First, don't put anything back in cartons or storage containers without making sure the box is clearly labeled on multiple sides. Clear plastic containers will help take some of the guesswork out of the process, too. Avoid making the boxes too heavy or stacking them too high. If they're too hard to move, you'll be tempted to let them stay where they are for good. Store only the items that intuitively make sense as belonging in your basement. Gardening tools, for instance, are better housed in your garage or shed. Segregate items so that like items are all in one place. Think of it as you would a retail store, keeping all kitchen items together in one spot, sports equipment in another, and so on.

Wednesday: Donate It

🕐 20 minutes

This is your chance to do a good deed while you make your basement a better place. As you sort through all the junk down there, keep an eye out for items that are perfectly good but that you just don't want anymore. Things that fall under this category might include that ice cream maker that you never took out of the box or that leather jacket you loved five years ago that fits a little too snugly these days. Anything you don't want that is not broken or damaged should be donated to your local Salvation Army or Goodwill; call them to come pick it up. You won't miss these items one bit, but someone else will be thrilled you let them go.

Thursday: Toss It

🕐 20 minutes

Your final pile is for your throwaways. Be sure to get rid of anything that's been damaged by humidity or pests. Now is also the time to dump anything that's obsolete, rusty, or not in working order. Lose the ceiling fan with the broken blade, the dot-matrix printer, and the coffee table with the bum leg. You probably have a few old cans of paint, varnish, and dried-up stucco there, too. Dispose of them, but make sure you do it in accordance with your local regulations. Visit your town or county's website to find out what to do.

Friday: Put It Somewhere Else

🕐 20 minutes

There are some items that simply do not belong in your basement, in large part because of the climate conditions. Dampness and sweaty walls are often problems, especially in older homes. And there's always a chance of flooding, so chemicals as well as items of special value should be stored above potential flood levels. If your basement is prone to high humidity or flooding conditions, move any precious mementos, books, letters, photo albums, and artwork to another area of your home. If you must store such items in the basement, make sure they're packed tightly in sealed plastic storage containers to keep out moisture and bugs.

Saturday: Shelve It

🕐 45 minutes

The basement floor is not the best place to store things. That is, after all, how you got into this mess in the first place. What you need instead is some shelving. If your basement is unfinished and has concrete walls, you'll probably want to go with freestanding shelves. If the walls are built out with studs and sheetrock, you can get wall-mounted shelving. When position-ing items on shelves, make sure the heaviest bottles, cartons, and cans are on low reinforced shelves, close to the floor. Place lighter and more frequently used items on the most accessible shelves—somewhere between waist high and eye level.

Sunday: Move the Bulk to the Basement

🕐 10 minutes

While there are many items that should not find refuge in your basement, there are others that are a perfect fit. For example, no matter how many doilies you lay on top of that 24-roll pack of toilet paper, it's never going to look pretty enough for dis-play in other parts of your home. This and other bulk items, such as nonperishable foods, paper towels, and light bulbs, can be stored on shelves in your basement. Stack items in a way in which you can easily see what you've got. Then you'll know when it's time to restock. This will also prevent you from buy-ing extras unnecessarily.

Basement Week 2

Monday: Make It a Family Affair

🕐 20 minutes

Basements make great family projects. Everyone in the home should have something invested in keeping that area in order. Prior to beginning to organize the basement, have a family meeting so that each member can consider what he or she might gain through a more organized basement. The chaos in the basement could be preventing your family from enjoying the space to the fullest, or maybe there's no room to store the things that actually should be down there. Not only does chaos make it harder to retrieve items when you need them, it can also prevent your family from spreading into these parts of the house. Could your basement provide a play room for small children or an entertainment area for older ones? If so, talk that up! You're likely to get more cooperation from your kids if they know that there is something in this project for them.

Tuesday: Set a Limit on Sentimentality

🕐 10 minutes

To get a clean basement, you have to play Bad Cop once in a while. As you and your family sort through items, your loved ones may have trouble parting with certain items for personal reasons. While it can be worthwhile to hold on to items of sentimental value, it's best to put some kind of system into place that will force you to be selective. For instance, create a memorabilia box for each family member. Limit the amount of items saved to what each person can fit in that box. Another idea is to take a picture of items that have sentimental value but you know will never have a place in your home. Instead of holding on to the actual item, you can hold on to the photo—or better yet, store the image on your computer.

Wednesday: Establish Zones

🕐 25 minutes

Are you abusing your finished basement by making it the whole-room equivalent of a junk drawer? Take a look around. The dumbbells are next to the laundry facilities, the tools have migrated to the arts-and-crafts area, and your holiday decorations are intermingling with your painting supplies. Instead of multiple-function areas, you have a mass of no-function areas. To redo the space you need to define it. Sit down and figure out how you'd ideally like to use your basement by breaking it up into zones. These might include exercise, laundry, TV and movie viewing, and children's play. Once you know what you want your basement to be, you can take the next step.

Thursday: Wine, Anyone?

🕐 15 minutes

Basements are a great place to store wine because of their darkness and cool temperature. If you have a collection, store bottles on their sides in a wine rack to prevent the corks from drying out. Also, make sure the bottles are a safe distance away from the furnace, hot water heater, and other heat-producing equipment. The last thing you need is for that bottle you're saving for your twenty-fifth wedding anniversary to explode before you can drink it. Group bottles by category: reds, whites, dessert wines, and so on. That way you'll be able to quickly locate the bottle you're looking for.

Friday: Lighten and Brighten

🕐 20 minutes

In many homes, unfinished basements are so uninviting they're downright spooky. Poor bare-bulb lighting, crumbly walls, and musty odors are the stuff of horror movies. Plus, unfriendly environments wind up contributing to storage problems and systematic disorganization. You run downstairs, toss an item on the pile, and run right up again. Imagine how much better off you'd be if you livened up the space. You don't need to sink much time or money in it. A quick whitewash would clean it up, and an upgrade to your lighting would brighten it up. To get more light, especially in the dark corners and halls of the basement, pick up a few inexpensive battery-operated lights, often used for closets. They're easy to install and require no wiring.

Saturday: Work It Out

🕐 20 minutes

Ever notice how home-gym gear like exercise balls and weights have a way of roaming? But with the right combination of storage aids, your equipment can always be within reach and within safety limits. Purchase a dumbbell rack or weight tree sized for the number of weights you have. Pop-up mesh cubes and baskets are good for containing odd-shaped gear like yoga mats, abdominal wheels, and resistance bands. For the ultimate in home-gym storage, there's the gym-in-a-box, an armoire with a built-in home fitness center disguised as an entertainment center. The doors open to reveal a treadmill and weight bench. There's even a shelf in there for a TV set. If you watch exercise videos on a secondary set while working out, store your fitness tapes or DVDs here, where you use them, rather than in the main TV viewing room.

Sunday: Prepare to Store

🕐 **30 minutes**

Once you've established what you want to store in your basement, begin to put away items in a neat and organized way. For example, clean, package, or launder the items beforehand. Polish your silver flatware before storing it. Items that go into storage in good condition are more apt to stay that way longer. Place items in appropriate (airtight) storage containers, which come in a variety of sizes. Also, mark each carton, container, or item with a descriptive label that's easily visible. For example, "Summer Clothing," "2008 Personal Financial Records," "Christmas Decorations," or "Winter Jackets." You want to store in such a way that your belongings can be easily found and retrieved without your having to dig through endless piles of stuff.

Basement Week 3

Monday: Store According to Use

🕐 **20 minutes**

As you decide where your various items will be stored in your basement (see "Establish Zones"), think in terms of when they'll be used. For example, you may want to store your winter clothing in containers near your holiday decorations. Likewise, you may want to store your grill near your Fourth of July decorations and lawn furniture. If you go on a family vacation every summer, you may want to store your luggage near your summer items for easy access. Your most frequently used items should receive prime storage space so they're most readily accessible any time of the year. If you also use your basement as a workshop, exercise room, or hobby area, make sure your storage area is kept separate. You can use room dividers or other methods to section off areas of your basement as needed.

Almost Perfect

Your basement is probably where all your important equipment is, like the furnace, water softener, water heater, and washer and dryer. Remember: these areas need to remain accessible for servicing. And that's not all. Clutter around these areas could create a fire hazard situation, so make sure the areas around pipes and drains aren't blocked with boxes.

Tuesday: Learn to Share

🕐 20 minutes

If you live in an apartment or condo, you might share your basement with other tenants or residents (if not, you get today off!). In this situation, you can still store your belongings, but you'll need to take a few precautions. When storing items in a communal storage facility, make sure you use containers that can be locked, especially if the area or storage cubicle you have access to is not totally secure. You'll still want to use airtight containers to store belongings such as clothing, books, papers, memorabilia, and so on, but you'll also want to take additional security precautions. For example, use containers that are opaque (not clear or see-through) and don't visibly label your containers. Instead, number them and keep the list of the contents of each numbered container to yourself. If someone happens to break into the communal storage space, you don't want to make it easier for them to find valuable items to steal or damage.

Wednesday: Bring in Plants That Like the Shade

🕐 15 minutes

If your basement is like most, it probably has those narrow little windows way up high as the only source of natural light. You may think that this makes live plants a nonoption for the basement, but that's not necessarily true. Certain species of plants actually thrive in deep shade or in indirect sunlight, such as jade plants and African violets. Pick out a few plants and a few decorative pots and place them near the windows, on wall-mounted shelves or tall furniture that puts them near the windows. This will add a little life to an otherwise gloomy basement.

Thursday: Use Garment Bags

🕐 10 minutes

The basement is a fine place to store hanging clothes that are not currently in season, but you need to take an extra step to keep them fresh and dust free. That step is a garment bag. You can buy these at any home goods store for anywhere from $5 to $10 each, and most garment bags can easily fit more than one item inside. Use these for winter coats, formal dresses, and any other garments you don't want to store upstairs in your closet. When you do bring something upstairs to wear, spray it with Febreze or throw it in the clothes dryer with a fabric softener sheet for twenty minutes to freshen it up.

Friday: Tie Up Both Ends of the Storage Spectrum

🕐 20 minutes

Large items like luggage and gardening equipment tend to end up in the basement because they don't fit anywhere else. It's fine if your basement's main purpose is storage, but you still want to do it in the smartest way possible. To make the best use of the space down here, nest any large items that you can. For example, put smaller suitcases inside larger ones, and stack flower pots and planters in size order. For smaller loose items like tennis balls and spools of ribbon, keep them contained in bins or lidded containers with labels on them.

Saturday: Lay It Down

🕐 30 minutes

If your lovely unfinished basement comes complete with a cold and ugly cement floor, a carpet might be just what you need to take it up a notch. However, this is probably not the place to lay down a plush family heirloom. Instead, go with something a little more rugged and durable. Measure the space and pick out some indoor/outdoor carpeting or pick out some Flor carpet tiles. You can cut the carpeting to fit your space and arrange the tiles any way you like. The great thing about Flor tiles is that you can replace them individually when they become damaged, which they're likely to be if your basement is used as a kids' playroom or a workout space.

Sunday: Try the Reflect Effect

🕐 15 minutes

We've already established that the basement can be a dark, spooky place. This isn't a big deal if you're just using it for storage, but if you plan to do any sort of activity down here—from playing Ping-Pong to folding laundry—you want to doll the space up a bit. To do this, hang mirrors on the walls or lean them up on surfaces so they can reflect whatever natural or unnatural light you have to work with. Just remember to keep the mirrors dusted and cobweb free to avoid that whole haunted basement look. Yikes!

Basement Week 4

Monday: Clear Out Cobwebs

🕐 10 minutes

Let's just cut to the chase. Cobwebs are gross, and just the threat of spiders is enough to make some people's skin crawl. Use the hose of your vacuum cleaner or a broom to clear corners of these dusty webs. Even if your basement is unfinished, it's still a good idea to do this every once in a while; you don't want to breed anything down there that will crawl upstairs to haunt you. It's a quick and easy chore that can be completed in minutes, and it'll do wonders for the look of your basement.

Almost Perfect

If you have one of those classic dark and damp basements, you may need a dehumidifier, which will clean the air and reduce mold-causing moisture. Just remember to empty the water receptacle as often as necessary.

Tuesday: Remove Broken Light Bulbs

🕒 5 minutes

As if basements aren't scary enough, you've just broken a light bulb while trying to replace it. Now it's dark as pitch, and there's shattered glass all over the floor. And the worst part is, the metal base of the light bulb is still stuck in the socket. What to do? First, turn off the light switch so there's no electricity running to the socket. Next, find a flashlight and clean up the glass. When that's done, go up to the kitchen and get a raw potato. Cut the potato in half, jam the cut side of one half over the shards of glass remaining in the socket, and twist the base out. Throw both the potato and the old bulb away when you're done.

Wednesday: Make Your Own Rags

🕒 10 minutes

As you sort through the old clothes and linens in your basement to determine which should stay and which should go, don't be too hasty about throwing things in the trash. Items that are too stained or damaged to be donated can often be used as rags. Convert ratty T-shirts to dust rags, and cut or tear old sheets into strips for any number of uses, from dishrags to padding for stored valuables. If a garment or piece of linen is completely gross, though, toss it. Trying to clean a surface with a filthy rag is an exercise in futility.

Thursday: Clear Out That Cardboard

🕐 20 minutes

If you're currently storing items in cardboard boxes in the basement, it's time to transfer them to something sturdier. In the event of a flood, cardboard will be useless, and it doesn't do much to keep bugs and pests out. What you need are a bunch of airtight, lidded containers. Clear plastic is best, as it allows you to see the contents without having to remove the lid, but opaque will be fine, too. Just make sure you label the outside of the container so you'll know at a glance what's inside. Label two sides but not the top, because you won't be able to see it if you're stacking. This will also help you remember to place a container in a certain direction when you put it back in its place. Finally, be specific when you label. Don't just write, "Holiday Decorations." Go with "Christmas Lights and Ornaments" instead.

Friday: Keep 'Em Separated

🕐 20 minutes

If you have a partially finished basement, place a clear divider between the storage area and the finished area. Folding screens or partitions work well to create separate rooms within your basement. An arts-and-crafts area won't be very relaxing if you can see lots of shelves and storage containers from where you sit. You also don't want the kids watching TV in the basement to be tempted to start rummaging through storage bins. Keep the two sides of your basement separate and you'll be better able to use each to its fullest capacity.

Saturday: Use Ceiling Space

🕐 **45 minutes**

Remember how you made use of the ceiling in other rooms of the house? You hung pots and pans from a rack in the kitchen (see "Hang It Up!"), and you strung up sports equipment in the kids' rooms (see "Cast a Net for Sports Balls"). It worked well, didn't it? Well, the idea that the ceiling is viable storage space holds true in the basement as well. If floor space is at a premium, or if you simply want to create a more open environment on your bottom-most floor, try hanging garden hoses, chairs, or lighting fixtures from joists in the ceiling. Avoid hanging items from pipes, though; the resulting stress could damage them, and a flooded basement is not a happy basement.

Sunday: Bag It!

🕐 **20 minutes**

If you choose to store sleeping bags, pillows, blankets, and other such soft items in the basement, you'll need to take an extra step to protect them from moisture and bugs. Luckily, this is easy as pie. All you do is stuff these items inside big, thick garbage bags and tie off the ends. If you use white bags, you can write the contents in permanent marker on the outside of the bag. Don't use up shelf space for these items. Instead, try to shove them in spots where other items won't fit, such as under the stairwell. Depending on how long you store bagged items in the basement, they may require some freshening when you retrieve them. In this case, just grab your trusty Febreze bottle and get the job done.

Basement Week 5

Monday: Phone Home

🕐 **10 minutes**

If you're the only person at home and the phone rings while you're folding laundry or using the treadmill, you don't want to have to race up the stairs to answer it. Instead, pick up an inexpensive cordless phone with charging dock and keep it somewhere handy—on an end table next to the couch or on a shelf in the laundry area. Perhaps you already have an extra phone you can just move down here. If so, this task will take you no time at all. You'll never miss a call again! But if you're down in the basement because you're trying to hide from your responsibilities, by all means let it ring.

Tuesday: Welcome Guests

🕐 **20 minutes**

In a perfect world, you could offer your out-of-town guests their pick of one of your many luxurious guest rooms in your sprawling mansion. This is reality, and you should count yourself lucky that you even have a basement to offer to your guests!

Seriously, though, it doesn't take much to transform a finished basement into a cozy guest room. A pullout couch, cot, or daybed is a great solution to the "Where should I put Aunt Peach?" problem. Even an air mattress will do in a pinch. The perks of the basement-as-guest-room plan are that it's super private, and the lack of natural light makes for a great night's sleep.

Almost Perfect

In a dark basement, time can sometimes cease to exist. You might dive into an organizational project down there and not realize how long you've been at it, causing you to miss dinnertime or your favorite TV show. While it's good to invest in the task at hand, don't overdo it. You have more important things to focus on. Set a timer to ding when you've worked for forty-five minutes or an hour. That way you'll make incremental progress toward the larger goal.

Wednesday: Don't Forget Photos and Artwork

🕒 10 minutes

Sure, it's a basement, but that doesn't mean it shouldn't feel like a part of your home. If you're going to be spending any significant amount of time down here, it's important to have some homey, personal touches around you. Display framed family photos or paintings, and go for a theme if you like. Many people use their finished basements as a display area for sports or music memorabilia or some other collection. If you have a pool, foosball, or Ping-Pong table down here, a sports theme would be a perfect fit. Be creative, have fun with it, and don't forget to let your kids in on the action.

Thursday: Take a Vow of Silence

(L) 10 minutes

The walls of your basement are obviously insulated by the ground, but the ceiling is a whole other matter. Sounds from above, like footsteps, music, and loud conversation, might travel through the floor to the basement really clearly—and basement noise can also travel up. If this is the case in your home, try to keep volume low in the spaces above and below the basement ceiling. To help insulate the space, add some standard pink insulation between the boards in the ceiling of your unfinished basement, or attach carpet remnants or old comforters to the ceiling. This will do the trick if you don't have the time to put in a proper ceiling right now.

Friday: Lock It Up

(L) 5 minutes

The metal double doors that lead out of your basement directly to the outside are a prime entry spot for burglars. And if someone gains access to your home through the basement, they can easily case your entire house. Even if you live in a safe neighborhood, get in the habit of keeping these doors locked just in case. Always keep these basement doors locked from the inside so you'll be able to get out if you need to in case of a fire or other emergency. If you lock them from the outside, thieves won't be able to get in but you won't be able to get out either!

Saturday: Create a Hideaway Home Office

🕒 45 minutes

If you're the type of person who's easily distracted while trying to get work done, your finished basement might be the perfect place for your home office or workspace. With windows too high to see out of, you won't be able to stare longingly out at the beautiful day or at your neighbors' kids playing catch in the yard. Because basement walls are underground, you also won't be distracted by the sounds of traffic, passersby, or the ice cream man making his rounds. If you have a big basement, you may be able to spread out more than you would in another area of your home. Give it a try and see if it works.

Sunday: Raise It Up

🕒 30 minutes

If your basement is prone to flooding, you want to make sure that any and all items that can be damaged by water are kept at least six inches off the floor. Wooden pallets, like those used in warehouses, are perfect for this. If you know anyone who works in a warehouse, ask if you can buy or have a few of these handy-dandy things. If not, go to your local hardware store and ask if they carry something similar. Buy pallets that can hold a lot of weight, as your washer and dryer are two heavy things you definitely want to keep clear of floodwaters. You don't want to add electrocuting yourself to your list of things to do.

ATTACKING THE ATTIC

When it comes to attics, most people apply the Utter Laziness strategy. Got something you don't know what to do with? Just throw it in a box, climb up the ladder, and shove it up there. In theory, this works. You clear your home of clutter and hide it somewhere out of sight. But in reality, you're creating a graveyard: a collection of outdated, broken, and forgotten objects that are taking up valuable space. Like it or not, it's time to take a trip upstairs—because attics don't have to be scary. Really.

Monday: It's All about Access

🕒 20 minutes

You can't organize your attic if you can't get into it, so you need to make your attic more accessible. Increased access will up the chances that you'll actually utilize and take care of the space. If you'll be using the attic as a storage area and will need to access it often, you might want to replace the basic access-panel entrance (which you may need a ladder to reach) with a pull-down staircase. Visit any hardware or home-improvement store to get help choosing one that will work for you. They might even install it for you—for a price.

Tuesday: Decide: Attic or Basement?

🕒 5 minutes

Your attic, basement, and garage are all areas made for storage, but each has its own identity when it comes to what should be kept there. For example, bulky, heavy items are best kept in the garage, as you won't have to go up or down stairs to bring them there or retrieve them. Consider what kind of items should actually go in your attic. Usually items that need a cooler climate should go in the basement, while those that are more weather-resistant can go in either the attic or garage. Also take into account whether any of these areas is susceptible to insect or rodent infestations. If so, keep all paper documents, photos, clothing, and other sensitive materials secured in airtight plastic containers. The last thing you want is to find that a mouse made a snack out of your precious family photographs.

Wednesday: Check the Weather

🕐 10 minutes

Most attics are not heated or air-conditioned, and you need to take this into account when choosing items to store here. For instance, clothing, linens, and photographs should not be stored in the attic unless they're kept in airtight bags or containers. With the potential for leaks, mold, insects, and rodents, you don't want to risk it. Lidded plastic storage containers are great for this (and relatively inexpensive). Make sure they're clear so that you can see the contents, but don't forget to label them as well.

Thursday: What Goes Up . . .

🕐 10 minutes

You know the rest. Anything that goes up into your attic is going to have to come down eventually. Permanent storage is a sign that your system has broken down. If you're in the habit of stowing items under the rafters and then immediately forgetting about them, it's a good bet that you don't really need them anymore. So throughout the attic-organization process, be critical about what you choose to store. Ask yourself if the items up there are even needed. If you haven't seen them or thought about them for years, it's time to say goodbye.

Friday: Consider the Possibilities

🕐 5 minutes

Can you use your attic for something other than storage? This is a swell plan, provided the space is big enough, well ventilated, and free of critters. But before you consider moving your teenager or "visiting" relative up to the attic, ask yourself a few questions about the space: Is there easy access to the attic? Is there ample headroom? Are there electrical outlets? If all of the basics seem to be in place, it might be just a matter of throwing down a rug, installing a fan, and adding furniture. Oh, and cleaning out all the clutter you've been storing up here for years.

Almost Perfect

If you think you don't want something but aren't sure, put it in a box that you store in the garage or attic. Label the outside of the box with the contents and the date. If you haven't used the item a year later, just donate the contents . . . and don't bother opening the box up again.

Saturday: Consult Your "No Use" Checklist

🕐 15 minutes

As you begin to sift through your attic storage, toss things that you don't have any use for. This list may include old tools that don't work, luggage that is broken or cumbersome, mildewed or damaged furniture, college textbooks (for most subjects, the material quickly becomes obsolete), old mattresses that are just collecting dust, appliances that no longer work or are rarely used, and cassette and VHS tapes (assuming you've joined the rest of the world and converted to CDs, MP3s, and DVDs). You won't have much luck selling or even donating most of these items, so just bite the bullet and toss 'em.

Sunday: Recruit a Crew

🕐 30 minutes

Warehousing items for friends, grown children, or other family members? This is as good a time as any to remind them about their belongings and invite them to join you in the reorganizing effort. "Invite" makes it sound like this is a pleasurable event, and in fact, these folks may have forgotten about their stuff and be excited to revisit it. Or they might just give you the green light to toss or sell their items. In any case, do your best to clear your attic of other people's belongings and furniture. Once you've done that, you can more easily assess your own items and decide which should stay and which should go.

Attic Week 2

Monday: Keep Out Critters

🕐 10 minutes

Yes, you love all God's creatures, but you don't need them in your attic. If you find signs that bugs or rodents have taken up residence on your top floor (such as droppings and webs), you need to take steps to evict them. When possible, use humane deterrents and traps. If these don't work, though, you'll have to pull out the big guns. We don't mean literal guns; that's a little on the violent side. Instead, pick up some mousetraps, rodenticide, pesticide, or whatever your problem calls for. If you don't have the heart for this kind of work, call in a professional. They should be able to eradicate the problem quickly.

Tuesday: Pack Your Bags

⏱ 20 minutes

No, you haven't won a surprise vacation. Sorry. Instead, we come bearing a great home organization tip! If you don't travel often but still keep several pieces of luggage stored in your attic, don't just let them sit up there empty. Fill those suitcases with items that need both storage and protection. Seasonal clothes are an option, of course, but you can also use luggage to store shoes, books, holiday gift wrap, and any other items you don't need to access frequently. The luggage should protect these items from getting dusty or becoming lunch for insects, and if you label the outside of each suitcase, you'll be able to tell at a glance what's inside.

Wednesday: Anticipate a Move

⏱ 20 minutes

If you think you could potentially be moving or remodeling your home in the next year or so, hang on to any boxes and packing materials that come your way. Flatten cardboard boxes and put them in garbage bags, or store them in the drawers of a dresser or armoire in your attic. Also save any bubble wrap and other cushioning material that might come in handy. Keep these up in your attic in a place where they'll be out of the way. Then, when it comes time to pack your things, you'll have the materials all organized and ready to go!

Thursday: Zip It Up

🕐 20 minutes

The attic is an okay place to store hanging clothes that are not currently in season, but you need to find a way to protect them from dust and critters. One option is a garment bag. Depending on how many coats, dresses, and other garments you're planning to store, you may need several of these. Luckily, they're fairly inexpensive and can usually hold more than one garment. Most garment bags zip shut to keep the garment completely covered, and some even come with mothballs or cedar hangers to help keep moths at bay.

Friday: Cobwebs in High Places

🕐 10 minutes

Most attics are A-frame structures, meaning they have roofs that are shaped like the letter A. (You learn something new every day, right?) Therefore, the highest point in your attic may be far out of reach. If you look up and see a tangle of dusty cobwebs up there, don't consider it a lost cause. Depending on how high your attic ceiling is, you may be able to reach those webs with a dust mop or broom. If not, you can buy an inexpensive extender pole at your local hardware store to make your mop or broom a few feet longer. Alternatively, dampen a couple of rags and simply toss them up into the rafters. Hopefully they'll collect some cobwebs on their way down.

Saturday: Label Your Bags

🕐 20 minutes

If you're storing any linens or blankets in your attic, they need to be protected from anything else that's walking around up there. So don't just start throwing rolled-up sleeping bags up there. First, take the time to make sure blankets or sleeping bags are clean to start out with; you don't want to be storing the mud from Billy's last camping trip in your attic. Then place them in garbage bags and tie them off. Throw a dryer sheet in the bag to make sure your blankets stay fresh. Label the bags, too, for easy identification.

Sunday: Shed Some Light on the Situation

🕐 30 minutes

Attics typically have only one or two tiny windows and are notorious for being dim, scary places. However, you can change this by adding some lighting to your top floor. Attics often have electrical cable running through them, so an electrician can easily tap into an existing circuit. Have him place the light switch near the entry for convenience, and select a switch with a warning light that reminds you when the light is on. If wiring a fixture and switch is too much trouble, or you don't want to pay to hire a professional to do it for you, install a pull-string light fixture yourself, preferably near the entry. If you want to take the absolute easiest way out of the darkness, though, just get a few battery-operated lights that can hang on the wall or sit near the entry.

Attic Week 3

Monday: Soften the Surface

🕐 20 minutes

Attic floors are not generally the most well-maintained in the house. Yours might have gaps between floorboards, nails popping up in places, splintered areas, and other spots where you can easily get snagged or injured. Luckily you don't have to redo the floors to take care of the problem. Instead, take a beat-up rug from another part of your house, or pick up some carpet remnants from the local hardware store, and lay those down in the areas where you walk most. If you have a lot of items stored in your attic, you might only have to cover narrow pathways. In this case, carpet runners will do the trick.

Tuesday: Spray Away Mustiness

🕐 10 minutes

Go to your local home goods store and find the beach/summer aisle. Don't get distracted by beach balls and Slip 'n Slides. Instead, pick up a spray bottle with a fan attachment on the end. These are usually battery powered and are meant for spritzing yourself with water to cool down at the beach. When you get home, unscrew the fan attachment and screw it onto your Febreze bottle, or simply pour some Febreze into the bottle you just purchased. Then walk around your attic dispensing bursts of freshness!

Wednesday: Fill Up Stored Furniture

🕐 **20 minutes**

That dresser, armoire, and bookcase are not just in your attic to take up space. You're storing them, of course, but there's no reason why you can't put them to good use at the same time. Use any available drawers and shelves to store other smaller items, such as books, artwork, clothing, sports equipment, and more. Just make sure you take proper precautions to protect those items that are fragile or targets for pests. Also consider labeling drawers with their contents so you can quickly look and know what's inside; you can make a list and place it right inside the drawer if you don't want to stick something on the outside of your stored furniture.

Almost Perfect

"Warning: Contents Under Pressure." Have you ever seen this warning on a product in a spray can? Don't take it lightly. Certain pressurized products, such as those that come in spray and aerosol cans, are extremely sensitive to heat and can explode in the wrong environment. Don't, for heaven's sake, store any such products in your stuffy attic!

Thursday: Wrap It Up

🕐 **20 minutes**

If you have a finished (or semifinished) attic, why not use it as an activity or task space? For example, if you keep a lot of gift-wrapping supplies in your attic, create a wrapping station up there. That way, you won't have to haul tubes of wrapping paper and spools of ribbon up and down the stairs every time you need them. If you decide to do this, try this handy setup: Slide tubes of wrapping paper and ribbon spools onto spring-loaded suspension bars that you can hang between rafters or tall pieces of furniture. Then it's just a matter of pulling out the length of paper or ribbon you want and cutting it with a pair of scissors. This works for rolls of tape as well. Lastly, make sure you also have a good surface, such as an old table, for wrapping gifts.

Friday: Clean Those Windows

🕐 **20 minutes**

We've already suggested a few ways to light up your attic, but if natural light is what you're after, try this one: clean the windows! It sounds simple, but it can make a huge difference. Attic windows are typically the most neglected in the entire house, with the exception, possibly, of basement windows. You'll be shocked to see how many layers of dust and grime come off when you wash them. Clean the insides of windows with glass cleaner and a rag, and if possible, spray the outsides with a hose. See how much brighter things look?

Almost Perfect

Out of rags? Use newspapers to shine windows. The ink will collect the dust and grime in seconds. You can also use newspaper to shine up a grimy stainless steel sink.

Saturday: Bring in Plastic Drawer Units

🕐 30 minutes

If ever there was an opportunity to use plastic drawer units, this is it. They're lightweight when empty, so they'll be easy to bring up to your attic, and once they're up there you can fill them with all types of items—from tools to craft supplies. The plastic will protect whatever is inside, and if you choose units with clear drawers, you'll be able to see the contents at a glance. If the drawers are opaque, add descriptive labels such as "Halloween Decorations" or "Summer Footwear." Place these units along walls where they'll be out of the way but where you'll still have room to open drawers fully.

Sunday: Get on Solid Ground

🕐 45 minutes

If you have a seriously unfinished attic—as in one that looks like the inside of a pink, fluffy cloud due to all the insulation— you need to do something to make the space more usable for storage. If you step on those pink spots, you risk going right through the ceiling below, so don't try it. Instead, bring up some sheets of plywood and lay them down over the joists. Do this in only as many spots as you need for entry and storage and leave the rest as is. Then just remember to step carefully when you bring up items to store. Also note that that lovely pink insulation is made of fiberglass and can irritate your skin, so steer clear!

Monday: Bring Old Briefcases Back to Life

🕐 10 minutes

Got any old briefcases lying around? Good! These make the perfect storage containers for lots of smaller items you store in your attic. It doesn't matter if the briefcases are out of style or a little beat-up. Because of their secure, latched design, you can safely store anything from paper documents to skeins of yarn inside and they'll be protected. We've said this before, but it's worth repeating: label the outsides of the cases so you'll know immediately what's inside. Store cases on a bookcase or in open-top bins for easy access.

Tuesday: Share and Share Alike

🕐 20 minutes

If you live in an apartment or condo and share an attic storage space, it's more important than ever to label all your items. In addition to marking down the contents of your storage containers, make sure you also include your name and contact information. That way if anything gets misplaced or damaged, folks can get in touch with you and let you know. And if you live in a large building and don't know all your neighbors, keep valuable items like bikes locked up. If you don't and someone walks off with something, you'll never stop kicking yourself.

Wednesday: Keep a Basket of Cleaning Supplies

🕐 10 minutes

You already know that certain cleaning products, such as those that come in pressurized cans, shouldn't be kept in a hot attic. However, there are other types of cleaning items you should keep on hand in case the dusting mood should strike you. Grab a big basket and fill it with a couple of rolls of paper towels, a canister of disposable wet wipes, and a clean rag or two. Plastic spray bottles of glass cleaner and oil soap are fine, too. If you keep this basket in the attic at all times, you won't be able to use the excuse that your supplies are downstairs to avoid cleaning. The key is to make chores as quick and painless as possible so you can get them done and then get back to your life!

Almost Perfect

When making decisions about what to keep in your attic and what to throw away or move elsewhere, you need to be, well, decisive! If you leave things up there, telling yourself that you'll come back to them in a few months, the clutter will build and build until you simply run out of room. Don't let this happen. Instead make decisions on the spot and act on them.

Thursday: Utilize Your Attic Closet

🕐 20 minutes

Huzzah! A closet in the attic is a rare gift, and if you have one, you have more options than most for how to organize items up there. You may choose to treat your attic closet the way you would any other closet in the house. Use it to store clothing, shoes, linens, and stackable boxes of smaller items.

Alternatively, you can give your attic closet a specific purpose. You might choose to store only camping gear here, or all of your sewing and craft supplies. That way you'll always know right where to go for particular items and will save time otherwise spent rummaging around.

Friday: Helpful Hampers

🕐 **10 minutes**

You have hampers in at least one or two rooms of your house. That's great, but you can use hampers to store items in your attic, too. Most likely you won't be disrobing up in your attic (unless you have a Peeping Tom you're trying to avoid), but there's plenty of stuff to put in them. Instead of holding dirty clothes, hampers in the attic can be used as storage bins for tall, thin items like tubes of wrapping paper, baseball bats, and umbrellas, or soft fluffy items like pillows, bedding, and sweaters.

Saturday: Avoid Holiday Horrors

🕐 **30 minutes**

Be sure to store your holiday decorations carefully so they'll be in good condition when next December rolls around. Store wreaths and coils of Christmas lights in suitcases and label the outsides with descriptions or photos of what's inside. You could also hang these items on your attic walls. Also, while you may have dutifully saved the box your artificial tree came in, that might not be the best bet for protecting your tree from bugs and other critters. Instead, pick up a durable Christmas tree storage container. These are typically long bags or boxes made specifically for this purpose. While it will require an up-front investment, you'll save money in tree replacements year after year.

Sunday: Fill Up the Trunk

🕐 **20 minutes**

We've advised you to use old trunks for storage in other parts of the house (see "Throw It in the Trunk"), but the attic might be the best place of all. Because your attic's entire purpose is storage, it won't matter if the trunk doesn't match your décor. Also, if the trunk is already up in your attic, you won't have to find a way to bring it downstairs. Just keep it where it is and fill it with items like bedding, pillows, seasonal clothes, and more. Just make sure the trunk has a good seal when closed; you don't want little critters making a nest out of your stored goods.

Almost Perfect

When people are coming over and you don't have time to clean, just do the floors, dust the tops of things (with a feather duster or microfiber cloths), and put out fresh flowers and candles.

FROM TOOLS TO TRICYCLES: THE GARAGE

You may not think of the garage as part of your home—or maybe you wish that it wasn't—but it and all the crapola in it belong to you. The tricky part is that a garage can take on a dozen different forms. Maybe yours is a workshop or a storage space, an auto repair center or a bike shop. Perhaps it's a hybrid, with different areas reserved for different functions. Whatever your garage situation, it's time to clean it out and clean it up.

Monday: Be Selective about Storage

🕐 20 minutes

Because your garage isn't a climate-controlled space, you'll want to be very selective about storing items there. Certain things, such as bikes, garden tools, and lawnmowers, are hardy enough to hold up in the garage. Others—including anything made of cloth or paper—should not be stored in the garage because of the possibility of mold and damage. Ideally you want to store less in your garage so that the few things you do store there will be readily accessible. So take a look around and separate the items that can stay and those that should go. Then split up the latter into two groups: items to store elsewhere and items to throw away or donate.

Tuesday: Make Sorting Simpler

🕐 15 minutes

Although it's best to wait to purchase storage until you know exactly what you'll need, it's wise to purchase at least a few inexpensive plastic bins (or even garbage cans) to store your items in while you're sorting. A little portable storage will make things easier as you work. These bins might ultimately become a useful component of your overall storage scheme. If you'd rather not make purchases yet, look around the house (or the garage!) for crates, boxes, or bins that will work in the meantime.

Wednesday: Keep It

🕐 20 minutes

What sort of items should you keep in your garage? Anything that is in good working order and that you use on a regular basis—or at least on a regular basis while it's in season. Some items habitually go into your garage year after year; as you sort, you should be able to identify these. You'll want to keep storing the majority of these in the garage, but for some, you may decide that the basement, attic, or shed is a better bet. Use your judgment and move items as necessary.

Thursday: Donate It

🕐 20 minutes

This is your chance to do a good deed while you get your garage in shape. As you sort through all the stuff you've been storing in there, be on the lookout for items that are in good shape but that you just don't want anymore. Things that fall under this category might include that pogo stick you thought was awesome a few years ago but haven't touched since, or that tricycle your kids have long grown out of. Anything you no longer use that is not broken or damaged should be brought to your local Salvation Army or Goodwill. You won't miss these items after they're gone, but someone else will be ecstatic to have them.

Friday: Toss It

🕐 20 minutes

It's time to be ruthless. Your garage is a finite space, and it simply can't hold every tool, vehicle, and piece of equipment you may want it to. If you find something that is broken, rusted, outdated, or otherwise damaged or defunct, just kick it to the curb. Don't hang onto items you think you might fix or refurbish one day, because chances are you won't. This isn't a personal judgment; it's just a fact. As time goes on, other projects will take up your time and attention and you'll forget all about that broken lamp you intended to rewire six months ago. Better to toss it now and make way for other items you're more likely to use.

Saturday: Clean It Out!

🕐 20 minutes

Today it's time to give your garage a good cleaning. Sweep out dust and dirt, pull down cobwebs, and possibly even hose down the floor. This doesn't have to take long; just give the garage a basic once-over so you have a semiclean slate to work with. If it's still a little dirty, just go with it! It's only a garage! There's no use in getting the floor clean enough to eat off of when you'll just be pulling the car in there soon.

Almost Perfect

If you have to fit two cars into a small garage, try this: Hang two tennis balls from fishing wire, each located where they will brush the center of your windshield as you pull in. This will help you get each car into the proper spot and prevent you from hitting anything that is stored along the back wall of your garage.

Sunday: Prevent Future Problems

🕐 20 minutes

Take a few minutes to make sure that your drains are clear and functioning well. Hosing off the floor will also give you the opportunity to check on the drain efficiency. If they're draining slowly or not at all, declog them before you put anything back into your garage. If your garage is attached to your home, a clog could cause flooding, so you'll want to attend to these drains even when they are just becoming slow but still function. A slow drain can quickly become a completely clogged drain.

Garage Week 2

Monday: Go After Grease Stains

🕐 20 minutes

Grease stains can usually be eradicated with one of two remedies: For set-in oil stains, pour cola over the oily areas and let it seep overnight. The following morning, lather some dishwashing liquid and water in a bucket. Rinse the cola with the soapy water and then hose it off. For fresh stains, add baking soda, cornmeal, or sawdust to the oily areas. The powder will absorb some of the oil. Then scrub with a brush or broom. Add automatic dishwasher detergent to the spot. (You do not need to rinse off the baking soda or sawdust.) Leave this mixture on the floor for several minutes and then pour boiling water over the area. Scrub with a stiff brush and rinse.

Tuesday: Get Rid of Pests

🕐 20 minutes

As you clean your garage and survey the items that have been stored there, take note of any signs of damage done by weather or pests. If there have been pests in your garage, you'll want to greatly reduce the number of items stored in your garage until you're able to identify the problem and solve it. Take note of which items attract pests and which ones suffer damage from the elements, and find a new home for these types of things. You are most likely to encounter evidence of pests in garages that haven't been properly sealed. The garage door is a point of entry for many little critters. The best way to check whether your garage door is sealing properly is to lie on the floor inside and look for light filtering in. Over several years, the rubber seal on the bottom of an automatic garage door does wear out, so you'll want to check the seal periodically.

Wednesday: Draw a Chalk Outline

🕐 20 minutes

After you've organized your belongings into categories, you'll want to begin to plan storage for the items you'll keep there. Keep your garage empty, and drive your car into it. Then take a piece of chalk and outline your car on the floor. Make sure you open the doors of your car to ensure that you leave ample clearance to get in and out of your vehicle(s). Finally, measure the remaining space to determine which types of storage might work for you.

Thursday: Put Everything in Its Proper Place

(L) 20 minutes

Do you have trouble keeping garage items in their proper places? Here's a trick that will solve the problem and get your kids involved. Work with your children to create a mini parking lot on the garage floor. You can use paint or heavy-duty tape to create "lanes" or "stalls" for various items. Not only will your items have specific homes in the garage, but your children will know where those homes are; they'll be able to put away their own bikes, scooters, and sports equipment. When you assign homes for every item, you'll eliminate the guesswork in putting things away.

Friday: Get Down Off the Shelves!

(L) 20 minutes

If you have shelves in your garage, keep in mind that items stored on shelves can attract children. Take some steps today to prevent little climbers from trying to scale the shelves. You can bolt shelves to the wall, and if you have a large storage component, you can make it extra safe by storing the heaviest things on the bottom and the lighter ones near the top. If you store a ladder in your garage, be sure to hang it horizontally to discourage children from climbing on it.

Saturday: Store the Smart Way

🕐 **20 minutes**

As you consider the best way to store items in your garage, think in terms of durable, hardy storage solutions, such as metal shelving and bins. For sports items, invest in a tension-mount storage rack. This will ease the strain on your bike's tires. If you store garden tools in your garage, purchase an upright tool organizer or mount yard implements (shovels, rakes, and brooms) directly to the wall. Because you won't spend much time in your garage admiring the aesthetics, focus on function when purchasing storage units for your garage.

Sunday: Seal That Floor

🕐 **1 hour**

To prevent oil spots, seal your garage floor. This makes it much easier to keep clean and will prevent future stains. Buy a standard concrete sealant from your local hardware store and pour the sealer in a paint tray. Use a paint roller to roll the sealer onto a clean floor. Slowly work your way out of the garage. Though you want to use a generous amount of sealant, make sure that you smooth out all puddles. Sealants can have a strong smell, so keep your garage door open and run a fan for ventilation. Do not apply a second coat of sealant, but do wash your tools quickly in a bucket of warm, soapy water.

Monday: Clean Out Your Car

🕐 20 minutes

If you keep your car in your garage—and really even if you don't—you should consider it a part of your grand organization. Even if your car is small, you can find clever spaces to store the items you need on the road. Many car manufacturers offer add-on accessories to make storing and transporting various items easier. Some of the most useful organization items you may want to add to your vehicle include a coin sorter (for toll money and parking meters), a holder for sunglasses, a cell-phone holder/hands-free kit, and a CD holder.

Almost Perfect

Buy a small crate or container to hold all your car necessities: tool kit, extra oil, winter scrapers, ice melt, windshield fluid, and so on. That way, all these things won't find homes rolling around in your trunk or under your back seat, and you'll know where they are when you need them.

Tuesday: Keep Records

🕐 20 minutes

In the glove compartment of your car, keep a maintenance log of all work that's done on your vehicle. In a file kept at home or in your car, keep copies of all maintenance and repair receipts, warranty information, and other related records. Each time you have work done on your car, ask when the next scheduled maintenance should be done. Mark your calendar to remind you what needs to be done and when. Also, try to get all of your car work done at a single location, whether at your local dealership, gas station, or mechanic. This will ensure that you don't overlap maintenance procedures or do maintenance that isn't necessary, such as replacing your car's air filter too often.

Wednesday: Get Help Keeping It Clean

🕐 20 minutes

If you have children, you probably find that these little folks add an extra layer of complexity to car maintenance. Luckily, they can also be your helpers. Train them to always carry their belongings from the car to the house when you get home. Consider setting aside a regular time each month for car care—if you need to, take it to the gas station and vacuum it out, or delegate this task to your spouse or older children. Although it can be costly, you might also want to have an annual "detail clean." If you can pay somebody else to attend to the deep cleaning, you'll have a far easier time managing the more mundane work of keeping the car orderly.

Thursday: Don't Dump That Old Fridge . . . Yet

🕐 20 minutes

Got an old fridge that still works fine but is languishing in your basement? Move that sucker out to the garage! Secondary fridges or freezers are great places to store bulk groceries you don't necessarily have room for in your kitchen refrigerator, such as six-packs of bottled water or soda or frozen meats. It's also a good idea to use this fridge for items you might want while you're working or relaxing outside, or when you're having a barbecue. These items might include beverages, hot dogs, hamburgers, popsicles, and anything else you might want at the ready. It's not laziness; it just makes sense!

Friday: Repurpose Old Furniture

🕐 **20 minutes**

Speaking of reusing old items you've got lying around, the garage is a great place to repurpose old but still sturdy furniture. Items you might consider bringing out to the garage instead of the curb include scuffed or nicked bookcases, lightly damaged dressers, old armoires, trunks you don't use, and extra buckets, bins, and garbage cans you don't have a use for in the house. You can use any or all of these to store tools, sporting equipment, barbecue supplies, and myriad other things you store in your garage. This will not only give old furniture items a new purpose, but it will also give you plentiful places to put things away.

Almost Perfect

If you store dangerous tools and chemicals in your garage, purchase storage that locks to keep children away from these hazards. You'll also want to install both a smoke detector and a carbon-monoxide detector in your garage and check them every six months to ensure they remain operational.

Saturday: Put Up Pegboards

🕐 **20 minutes**

Pegboards are a garage organizational system that never goes out of style. These are great for storing tools and other items so that they're both neat and easy to grab as needed. Pick up a precut pegboard, or have one cut to size, at your local hardware store, and then use it to hang whatever you want. By attaching hooks to the ends of tools, you can hang them singly. You can also hang sports equipment, pool accessories, and toys so they're off the floor. A simple solution for bulky items like soccer balls and baseball mitts is to place them in mesh bags and then hang them on a pegboard hook.

Sunday: Reuse Washable Containers

🕐 10 minutes

Need a place to keep all those random screws, nails, washers, bolts, nuts, pushpins, and other tiny items in the garage? Clean and set aside a bunch of peanut-butter and jelly jars, yogurt cups, plastic juice bottles, and other containers that can be used to store small items. Use clear glass or plastic containers when possible, or label the outside so you know what the contents are. Store the filled containers on shelves or in cabinets for easy access to the things you need. And when you find a screw or nail lying around, don't toss it in a junk drawer; put it in its proper container. You'll be surprised how nice these items can look when they're kept neat and organized.

Garage Week 4

Monday: Listen Up!

🕐 15 minutes

If you'll be spending a lot of time in your garage—working on your car or other projects, perhaps—why not add a soundtrack to your space? Bring a music player, such as a radio, CD player, or MP3, player out to the garage and put it someplace where it won't be in danger of damage. Don't bring your brand new, highly expensive stereo out here. The chances for damage by the weather or reckless kids are just too high. Stick with an older, inexpensive unit that you can place on a shelf or affix to the wall to keep it out of the way. And if electrical outlets are few and far between, a battery-operated device might be best.

Tuesday: Hose Down Screens

🕐 15 minutes

The garage is a good place to store window screens for the winter, but when you pull them out for summertime, they're likely to be a bit dusty and covered in cobwebs. Today, take all the screens out onto your lawn and lean them up against a few tree trunks or a fence, then give them a good spray-down with the hose. This will clean off any dust, dirt, and cobwebs, and the pressure of the water will clear out any areas of screen that were clogged. When you're done, just let your screens air-dry. When you put them back on the windows, you'll have nice, fresh air blowing into your home, cooling you off all summer long.

Wednesday: Love Your Lawn Mower

🕐 20 minutes

If you care for your lawn mower and store it properly, it will be in good condition year after year, so start the process today. If you use an old-fashioned manual lawn mower (the kind with blades that rotate as you push it), simply clean it up at the end of the season, spray the blade and points of rotation with a household lubrication oil, like WD40, and store the mower so that no metal parts are in direct contact with the garage floor. If you have a gas-powered or electric push or riding mower, empty the clipping collectors, give the mower a good wipe-down with a damp cloth, and store it on a raised surface where it won't get wet in the event of flooding. In the spring, take your mower to a professional for a full cleaning, blade sharpening, and lubrication job.

Almost Perfect

Get your bicycles out of the line of foot traffic in your garage. Mount them flush to the wall and add an additional rack for helmets and other accessories.

Thursday: Avoid Paint Popsicle

🕐 **20 minutes**

Cans of paint are best stored somewhere other than in your non–climate-controlled garage. If you leave them out there all winter, you'll end up with paint popsicles. Some paints can survive one or two freeze-thaw cycles without harm, but not all. Here's how to tell if paint has been irreparably damaged: Thaw the paint, open the can, and stir. If it appears smooth and creamy like new paint, it's probably fine. If the contents have separated and can't be easily mixed or if there are lumps and a grainy texture, it's time to toss it. Dispose of chunky paint according to your town's waste disposal laws and start anew.

Friday: Get Big Items Up Off the Floor

🕐 20 minutes

Consider whether anything in your garage that takes up significant floor space can be mounted and stored on the wall. Examples include bags of golf clubs, bicycles, tennis rackets, snow shoes, skis, and even wheelbarrows. There are all sorts of mounting systems on the market; depending on what you want to hang, you should be able to find the right one for your needs. You can also hang netting or wire cages to hold sports balls and other oddly shaped items. Once these items are up off the floor, you'll have more space for the things that can't be mounted (like the car), and you'll be able to easily see and access what you've got.

Saturday: Love the Four Seasons

🕐 45 minutes

If you live in a four-season climate, you probably have plenty of things that go in and out of your garage in a seasonal rotation. Today, make sure there's room for everything. If you store your patio furniture inside for the winter, the ceiling rafters are an ideal place. Open, adjustable rafter shelves can be attached to the roof truss of your garage. Not only that, they can handle car seats, camping gear, and ski equipment, among other things, without getting in the way of your parked vehicles. If your garage is tall enough, you might even think about constructing a storage loft area using a bunk bed–style ladder to access it.

Sunday: Sell Your Stuff

🕐 1 hour

Throwing away junk and donating good items that you don't need is definitely the name of the game when it comes to cleaning out your garage. However, if you have a bunch of more valuable items and are looking for a way to make an extra buck, consider selling your stuff. You can have a garage sale, or if you don't feel like putting in the effort, just sell your stuff online. Post your items on Craigslist or eBay or offer them up on your Facebook page. You can also put an ad in your local paper and wait for local shoppers to flock to you. At the end of the day, you'll have a bunch of cash and a lot more space in your garage.

Garage Week 5

Monday: Hook It Up

🕐 10 minutes

Heavy-duty hooks are indispensable in the garage. These can be mounted on wallboards and used to store anything from aluminum folding ladders to coiled extension cords. The key to using these hooks is to make sure you don't overburden them. Most hooks will come labeled with a weight capacity, which you should adhere to. Don't tell yourself, "Eh, it'll probably hold." It's not worth the risk of your brand-new bike or electric drill plummeting to the cement floor—or worse: landing on your car! Follow the instructions for installing hooks so they'll be as sturdy and reliable as possible.

Tuesday: Use Your Year-Round Garage

(L) **30 minutes**

If you have a heated and insulated garage, you are one lucky duck. Consider using half the space for your car and general storage and the other half as a year-round recreation area. For instance, you might decide to lay down some durable indoor-outdoor carpeting and add a Ping-Pong table, a dart board, or a table and chairs for board games, crafts, and other activities. There's no reason you can't decorate this area a little bit, too. Hang up some strings of white lights or lanterns for a festive look, and hang some art or other items on the wall. Street signs or old-fashioned light-up signs (such as neon beverage advertisements) might make fun additions to your garage's decorating scheme.

Wednesday: Group Seasonal Items Together

(L) **20 minutes**

One way to keep your garage neat, clean, and organized is to group seasonal items together. For example, store all winter-related tools and equipment in one area. These might include shovels, car scrapers, winter sports gear, buckets of rock salt, and so on. Spring and summer items might include the lawn mower, rakes, fertilizers, gardening tools, and warm-weather sports equipment. Make sure items have assigned places so you and your family can put them away easily after use.

Thursday: Clean Up for Camping

🕐 20 minutes

If you and your family are avid campers, you probably have loads of gear reserved specifically for that purpose. These might include tents, a camping stove or grill, citronella candles and/or tiki torches, camping chairs, mess kits, and any number of other items. For easy retrieval and use, keep all your camping items together, packed in their individual carrying cases and combined into larger bags or bins when possible. Then, when a camping trip comes up, you can simply load up your car and hit the road!

Friday: Set Up the Grill

🕐 10 minutes

If you like to barbecue in the summertime but don't want to leave your grill outside where it can rust in the rain, you're likely storing it in your garage when it's not in use. The problem with this is that it might not be that easy to move in and out. If your grill is old or broken, consider replacing it with a newer model on wheels. This will make rolling it in and out of the garage a snap. If your grill is in good shape but tough to move, place it on top of a wheeled pallet so you can simply roll it out into the driveway or yard when you want to use it. Also keep grill tools clean and close by for easy retrieval.

Saturday: Don't Dim the Lights

🕐 1 hour

If you spend a lot of time in your garage, good lighting is essential. Puttering around in the dark is a recipe for disaster, so make sure you have proper lighting in all areas. If you use your garage mainly to house your cars and store items, lighting from incandescent bulbs will be sufficient. Incandescents come on immediately, use very little energy, and will not flicker like some cheap fluorescents no matter how far the temperature drops. However, if you use your garage as a workshop or some other kind of activity center, high-quality fluorescents are a better bet. Fixtures with T8 tubes and electronic ballasts are worth the extra expense over standard fixtures. (FYI: T stands for "tubular," and the number refers to how many eighths of an inch are in the diameter—in the case of a T8, one inch.)

Sunday: Get in the Water

🕐 20 minutes

Do you and your family members spend so much time in or on the water that you wish you had gills? If so, a neat and orderly collection of aqua sports gear and equipment is a necessity. Since this stuff can take up lots of space, come up with ways to make it more compact. For example, if you have a canoe or kayak, store items like lifejackets, oars, and fishing poles right inside it. Also make any large items smaller when possible. This includes letting the air out of any inflatable rafts, tubes, and other flotation devices. Fold up the deflated items and keep them someplace where they'll be safe from bugs and other hazards. When you're ready to ride the waves, just grab the items you need and go!

Afterword

MAINTENANCE IS NOT A FOUR-LETTER WORD

You've cleaned every room of your house, looked your clutter demons in the face, and implemented new organizational strategies that have helped you move into a cleaner, brighter, happier future. And you've been spending more time with your friends, going to the park more often with your dog, and taking the time to pay more attention to your kids and their needs. As you continue to better manage your home and time, keep in mind that your home is a work in progress. It's not perfect—and it never will be. Instead it's filled with family, friends, and love. Yes, there's a dust bunny or two under your bed, but who cares! All you have to do now is keep up what you started.

Celebrate Success

Home organization is not a prison sentence for your cleaning crimes of the past. You're doing all this cleaning and organizing for you and your family, and when you achieve a goal, you should celebrate it. If you've worked for the last several weeks to give your dining room a facelift, invite friends and family over for a celebratory dinner. If you've been working to clear off your deck or patio, invite your neighbors over for a barbecue. The compliments you receive on your work will make you feel proud and will motivate you to tackle the next project.

As you complete your goals and celebrate your successes, always keep in mind that home organization is not separate from the rest of your life. Putting dishes away after dinner, placing books you read back on the shelf, and folding and putting away clothes that have just come out of the dryer are just preparations for the next adventure life is going to bring your way. Take small steps toward big goals, and you'll never find yourself overwhelmed or discouraged. Let a neat, orderly home (and maybe a cupcake or two) be your reward, and you'll always be able to find the motivation to move forward.

THE "HOLY CRAP! COMPANY'S ON THEIR WAY" 10-MINUTE QUICK-CLEAN PLAN

Your Mother-in-Law/best friend/sister calls and says she's on her way over and all you can think is, "Holy crap! The house is a mess!" Chill out. These tips will help you create an illusion of clean and tidy in no time.

1. If you don't have time to give your bathroom a thorough scrub, just Windex the mirrors and the top of the sink. Give your toilet a quick scrub and you'll be good to go!

2. Spray your furniture and rugs with Febreze to freshen up your living room in seconds!

3. Brighten up your woodwork by running a furniture polish-soaked rag over anything that looks dusty. You'll not only get rid of dust, you'll make the room smell clean to boot.

4. Throw any loose clutter in a basket that you'll go through later. Baskets are attractive—and easy to hide.

5. Change out the towels—especially the hand towels—in your bathroom and use the old ones to wipe down anything that's covered in dust or grime.

6. Throw your dishes in the dishwasher. Getting stuff off your counters and out of your sink makes your kitchen look cleaner almost instantly.

7. Close any open doors. That means cabinet doors, closet doors, and doors to rooms you didn't have time to clean.

8. Place a fabric softener sheet on the backside of an oscillating fan in any room in your home. (The force of the air will make it stick.) As the fan cools down the room, it will also infuse the air with the scent of clean laundry.

9. Nothing makes your living room look neat and clean like a newly vacuumed rug, so grab your Hoover and go to town.

10. Relax. If you act like you're more interested in your guests than in the stuff you didn't pick up or the room you didn't dust, your guests will focus more on you too.

INDEX

ABOUT THE AUTHORS

I. B. Caruso is an award-winning writer who covers home style, design, and real estate. Her lifestyle articles have appeared in the *Wall Street Journal*, BobVila.com, *Natural Home*, Front Door.com, and several in-flight publications, among others. She lives in Long Island, NY.

Jenny Schroedel has written countless articles on all aspects of cleaning house—financial, emotional, and practical—and how they work together to create a happy, healthy, organized home. She lives in Chicago, IL.

Getting Where Women Really Belong

- Trying to lose the losers you've been dating?
- Striving to find the time to be a doting mother, dedicated employee, and still be a hot piece of you-know-what in the bedroom?
- Been in a comfortable relationship that's becoming, well, too comfortable?

Don't despair! Visit the Jane on Top blog—your new source for information (and commiseration) on all things relationships, sex, and the juggling act that is being a modern gal.